generation

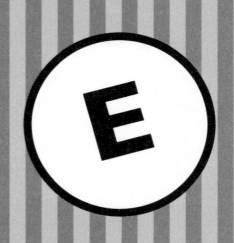

generation

<entrepreneur>

The Do-It-Yourself
Business Guide for
Twentysomethings
and Other
Non-Corporate
Types

JOEL AND LEE NAFTALI

Ten Speed Press
Berkeley, California

1➋

Ten Speed Press
P.O. Box 7123
Berkeley, California 94707

A Kirsty Melville Book

Distributed in Australia by E. J. Dwyer Pty. Ltd., in Canada by Publishers Group West, in New Zealand by Tandem Press, in South Africa by Real Books, in Singapore and Malaysia by Berkeley Books, and in the United Kingdom and Europe by Airlift Books.

Design by Catherine Jacobes

Library of Congress Cataloging-in-Publication Data
Naftali, Joel
   Generation E: the small business start-up guide for twentysomething entrepreneurs and other corporate rejects / Joel and Lee Neftali.
       p. cm.
   Includes bibliographical references and index.
   ISBN 0-89815-897-4
   1. New business enterprises.   2. Small business--Management.
I. Naftali, Lee.   I. Title.
HD62.5N33   1997   96-54222
                                          CIP

First printing, 1997
Printed in Canada

1 2 3 4 5 6 7 8 9 10 — 00   99   98   97

For Janis:
A dear friend, a sweet soul,
and a brain on wheels.
Rest easy.

Contents

Acknowledgments

THANKS TO Christa Laib for saving us from the dreaded slush pile, and to Kirsty Melville and Mariah Bear at Ten Speed for their keen ability to spot a diamond in the rough. Thanks to Nigel and Mom for their input. And special thanks to Mom, Dad, and Mom: Without their constant support and generosity, this book would be just another file in our "Possible Projects" folder.

Introduction

Help! Our Standard of Living Has Fallen and We Can't Get Up

WE'VE ALWAYS HATED INTRODUCTIONS that explain the problem the book is supposed to solve. If the readers didn't know what the problem was, they wouldn't be reading the book in the first place. So we'll restrain ourselves, and won't paint a desperate, painful picture of the job market that faces the young, the alternative, the principled, the passionate, and all the other corporate rejects. You're reading this—you know how bad it is.

So just imagine that we've discussed the declining median income for people in their twenties and thirties, the preponderance of temporary and part-time work in the "jobless recovery," and the unfortunate fact of the Baby Boomers, who have squatted solidly in those mid-level jobs that are the goal of all entry-level wage slaves. Pretend that we've passionately decried the mind-numbing, soul-eating, life-sucking agony of spending forty hours a week doing something you hate just so you can make barely enough money to cover food and rent.

Instead, we'll jump right in and start talking about the solution—self-employment.

Self-employment is good. You can be the boss. You can make a higher-than-embarrassing wage. You can do something you're proud of. Of course, there are some risks: you can fail, go bankrupt, and have to start all over again. And there are all kinds of obstacles: lack of money, lack of an innovative business idea, lack of business savvy, and so on.

These obstacles can seem insurmountable, but you've already overcome one of the most difficult of them: imagining that starting your own business might—just possibly might—be the right thing for you. You've also bought this book (haven't you?), which will reduce your downside risks and help you overcome all obstacles with near-miraculous results.

So set aside all your assumptions about the soulless world of business. Ignore that niggling notion that we are not writing these words for you, because you don't know the first thing about business. Listen, if you have $50,000 in the bank, have owned three business that are now being traded on the New York Stock Exchange, and own the patent rights to the Ultimate Mousetrap, you don't need this book. (In fact, give us a ring—we have an investment opportunity for you.) But if you have no money, no business experience, and no idea what sort of business you'd start even if you *did*, this book is for you.

It may not make you rich (not quick, anyway), and it may not transform you into a giant of commerce, but this book will give you *all* the information you need to create a small, viable business. A business that, at the very least, pays better than what you'd get working some demeaning office job for an impersonal corporation. A business in a field that interests *you*, that meets *your* needs, that you're *passionate* about. A business in which you make the decisions, that is run the way you think a business ought to be run. And a business that—and this may come as a bit of a shocker—is challenging, stimulating, creative, fun, and even outrageous.

Well, them's fighting words. But can we deliver? *How* will we deliver?

We can. We'll deliver in four quick and easy steps: We'll talk about you, we'll talk about business ideas, we'll talk about how your business can actually make money, and we'll talk about all those fiendish details that you can't avoid.

PART ONE: FIND YOUR PASSION AND TRANSFORM IT INTO A BLUEPRINT OF YOUR PERFECT BUSINESS

First, we'll make some assumptions. You're not *too* stupid—maybe you're even bright. You suspect that working for yourself, despite all the risks (hell, maybe *because* of them), is a better long-term plan than growing dim and bland working under the fluorescent lights of a corporation that gives you nothing but a weekly envelope. You possess some ungodly mixture of chutzpah, animal cunning, and doe-eyed innocence. You know nothing about business and are, you think, totally unprepared to join the shark-infested waters of capitalism and naked greed.

You in a nutshell, right?

The first problem is this: you probably have no idea what you're looking for in a business. You might feel you have some formless talents, some undifferentiated skills and abilities, but absolutely no clue what you ought to use them for. (Even if you are one of those rare-but-annoying people who was born knowing what you want to do, stick around. You might learn something.)

So the first thing we'll do is help you discover your Guiding Principle. Yes, this is one of those "follow your bliss" things. But there's a twist. You're young (or young at heart) and you're clueless. When you're young and clueless (and we speak from experience), you don't have to feel that once you find your guiding principle it's carved in stone forevermore.

This is important. There are plenty of books that help you find your purpose, and most of them give the terrifying impression that once you find it, *that's it*. You've found your *reason d'être*. You'd better work on that one thing for *the rest of your life,* or you're just fooling yourself.

Nonsense.

We *will* help you find your guiding principle (or passion, mission, whatever). If you follow our wise advice, you'll discover something that you enjoy doing, that you do well, that you get excited about. And something that you can get *totally, irrevocably, entirely* committed to (until you decide to do something else).

This finding-your-guiding-principle stuff does not commit you forever. We're looking for something you can commit to for some real length of time, say one year, or three years, or even (gasp!) ten years. We've started a business doing something we didn't care about at all, and made a little money (but, unsurprisingly, we didn't have all that much fun). But when you start a business you really care about, it's just that much easier to make it a personal and financial success.

Next, we'll talk about your resources. Don't snicker—we know you have some. Your resources include friends you can impose upon, your '82 Chevy Impala that barely runs, all the people you know from your AA meetings, the $400 of credit on your 25 percent interest rate credit card, your glib and silver tongue, and much, much more! Just stay tuned, and you'll learn all about exploiting, er, discovering your resources.

Then it gets exciting. We tie it all together and use your guiding principle and resources to give you a broad outline of your ideal business.

PART TWO: MORE THAN 300 BUSINESSES YOU CAN START OR CUSTOMIZE

Part Two is about filling in that broad outline.

Now that you know all about your deep inner desires, we'll take you on a walking tour of low-cost business ideas. We've included hundreds of businesses that focus on the environment, art, crafts, health, animals, music, writing, computers, plants, and other interesting stuff.

All you've got to do is browse through the Business Idea Directory and note all the business ideas that mesh well with your guiding principle. And then note all those ideas that catch your fancy for no reason at all. You'll end up with a list of business ideas that you can use as starting points when developing your own one-of-a-kind, perfectly customized business.

Or, if customization isn't your thing, you might be pretty happy starting a business that's more or less exactly like one we list in the Business Idea Directory. The only real difference between the two approaches is the degree to which you personalize your business.

And even if you're the least innovative of entrepreneurs (which we doubt), you'll have to do *some* personalization. Every small business must be unique—it has to respond to different opportunities and risks and resources. After you scan through the Business Idea Directory, we'll show you how to squeeze as much juice as possible out of the ideas that appeal to you. We'll show you how to expand, limit, adapt, combine, substitute, and otherwise twist your ideas to fit your whim and your guiding principle.

Then you'll have a business idea perfectly tailored to your needs and resources. One big question remains: Will anyone pay you for such a thing? There's only one way to find out: market research.

PART THREE: MARKETING, OR FROM PASSION TO PROFIT: MAKING YOUR BUSINESS A MONEY MAGNET

Market research is an unfortunate business startup necessity, but it *is* a necessity. You might decide to do as little research as you can, and that's okay. Just do some. Starting a business with no market research is like using the rhythm method for birth control: It *might* work. We'll show you how to test if your small business dreams have any hope of coming true.

If they do, you'll have to make a plan. Don't worry—your business plan will be short and informal. Its only purpose is to help you develop a successful business, not to sell your business to a bank manager or venture capitalist. It will tell you how to start your business and how to set it up so you actually make a profit. But it won't tell you how to bring in cash. For that, you need marketing.

Many business owners confuse marketing with advertising, and think it's expensive and ineffective. Or they confuse it with selling, and think it's scary and manipulative. But marketing is bigger than advertising and selling—marketing is whatever you do to create customers. Advertising and selling are just a couple of well-known and (usually) ill-used marketing techniques.

But you'll know a lot more than two marketing techniques when we're done. And you'll know how to use them to get the most possible profit with the least possible expense, too. We're not going to pretend that having no money is always a benefit for a business startup. But having no money can be a pretty good thing when it comes to marketing. You won't rely on an inane ad campaign, because you can't. Instead, you'll have to rely on your ingenuity, determination, and an array of highly effective, low-cost marketing techniques. And those three things, taken together, can create a marketing campaign as effective as any amount of money. You've got the ingenuity. And you've got the determination. All you need now is the marketing techniques. What a coincidence. We've got them.

We don't know what kind of business you'll be starting. So we've included all the most affordable and effective marketing techniques we could find in the marketing chapter. Go through them and decide which will work best for your business and your personality. The goal is to choose as many techniques as you can use consistently, comfortably, and effectively.

Once you choose the best marketing techniques for you, it's just a matter of putting them together to create a simple marketing plan. This is an absolutely vital step that the majority of small business owners never take—and then they wonder where all the customers are. Your business will be different. Unlike those clueless folks, you'll know exactly what you're doing, and exactly where your customers are. And you'll profit from the knowledge.

PART FOUR: THE DETAILS, OR THE QUICK AND EASY GUIDE TO ACCOUNTING AND TAXES

We threw this section in because our accountant told us that we had to. Well, okay, actually this is all vitally important stuff. Unfortunately. But although it's boring to learn, much of it, in the hands of a properly savvy business owner, provides an objective method for understanding your business. And when it comes to your business, objectivity is hard to come by.

So what is this wondrous provider of objectivity? Bookkeeping.

We know—you can't even balance your checkbook, much less post your income and expenses, develop a profit and loss statement, and choose between the cash and accrual methods of accounting. Don't worry. We've got a simple plan to help you do the minimum necessary to keep your books.

And there are two reasons why you must keep your books. First, they provide a tremendously helpful snapshot of the condition of your business. They'll show you if money is coming in or going out, and help you do what you can to keep things moving in the right direction. And second, the IRS says you must keep books. If you don't, they can grind you into a fine paste.

Then there's taxes. Paying taxes isn't so bad—it means you had a profit. On the other hand, it's better to keep your money in your pocket instead of supporting the military-industrial complex. We'll discuss a little of that. Mostly, though, you've got to know enough about taxes to keep from getting stomped by the IRS. That's just about as much as we'll be showing you.

So there you have it:

- Discovering your guiding principle and resources.

- Selecting interesting business ideas from the directory.

- Personalizing your business ideas and making a business plan.

- Developing a winning marketing strategy.

- Understanding all the nasty financial details.

By the time you finish this book, if you religiously follow our advice, do the exercises, and watch your posture, you'll have a viable business startup idea, a plan for turning that idea into a thriving business, and the know-how to implement the plan.

At this point, we're supposed to say, "There's only one thing you have to bring along: you. Without your determination, enthusiasm, belief in yourself, blah blah." You've heard it. It's true, but boring.

So we won't say that. Instead, we'll say, "The juggernaut of the U.S. economy will no longer bear you along in its wake if you simply show up for work with the right piece of paper, the right accent, or the right body temperature. You can whine all you want about this and sit around getting nowhere. Or you can whine all you want about it and take the leap into self-employment."

We're not going to tell you that running your own business is going to be easy. Hell, we're not even going to tell you your business will be a financial success.

But what options do you have? You could take a huge risk with a great idea, an idea you're proud of and excited about, and possibly fall flat on your face; or you can shuffle along in a mediocre life of soul-eating drudgery, complaining that life isn't fair. You pick.

Let's say the worst happens. You take the huge risk of starting your own business—you put all your money, all your self-esteem, all your hopes on the line—and your business fails. Well, here's a big secret: you're still better off than that brain-dead zombie who never even tried.

And here's an even bigger secret: there is absolutely no reason you won't eventually succeed. Yes, "eventually" is the catch. But this book will get you up and running stronger and faster than 99 percent of the other businesses out there. Keep at it—you *will* succeed.

Find Your Passion and Transform It Into a Blueprint of Your Perfect Business

PART ONE

Finding Your Guiding Principle, or No More "Fries with That?"

Q: What is an airy-fairy "find your passion" chapter doing in a business book?

A. Because it's an airy-fairy business book.

B. Because there are plenty of other books out there that'll tell you all about (and *only* about) money, profit margins, and the bottom line.

C. Because the most practical, fun, and profitable business you can possibly start is one that absolutely thrills you.

Well, all of the above, actually—with a heavy emphasis on "C." But it can be tough to discover what will thrill you. You'd probably be pretty happy being your own boss, making your own decisions, working your own hours, and getting paid what you're worth in any number of businesses. One of the benefits of this book is that it will help you attain all that in whatever business you choose. But *thrilled?* That's a different story.

That depends on how you love to be, what you love to do, and what you love to do it to: that's your guiding principle. Once you find that, you have a target to aim for and a standard to measure decisions and accomplishments against. So if your guiding principle involves creativity or uniqueness, for example, you'd better think twice if you're offered a wonderful opportunity running a rigidly organized franchise, and instead look at businesses that involve design or art.

In this chapter, you'll find your guiding principle. You'll establish the goal that will pull you toward success. We're not talking about specific business decisions right now, we're talking about *you*, about choosing an activity that you'll find fulfilling and exciting. We'll worry about transforming that activity into a successful business in a later chapter.

If you already know exactly what business you're going to start, you still ought to read this chapter and do the exercises. Every business can be operated in an incredible variety of ways. You want to run yours in a way that is as congruent with your guiding principle as possible. Not only is this the easiest and most enjoyable way to organize your business, but it'll turn out to be the most profitable way as well.

The same holds true if you are "only" interested in starting a business as a money-making prospect. That's fine. But just because you don't especially want to invest your soul in an industrial abrasives business—which you think will pay well, though you're not too excited about viscosity and grit—doesn't mean you won't benefit by knowing your guiding principle. Even the most mundane business can be transformed into something you genuinely care about, and usually without too much effort.

Unfortunately, the world of business doesn't exist solely to cater to your every whim—profitability is important as well. We know that, you know that, and in later chapters we'll work out how to extract as much as possible from your guiding principle while still keeping a steely eye on the bottom line. But for now, don't worry about how it's all going to come together—it *will* come together, and probably much better than you think possible. That said, let's get to work.

The techniques we present do work. If you're like us, and think you can get all the benefit of the exercises by skimming through them without actually doing anything, we urge you to return this book to the bookstore right now, while it's still in good condition.

That said, remember that you don't have to get the exercises perfect—just get them done. You could spend weeks doing all the exercises in this book. Don't. Just do as little or as much as feels right, as long as it's more than nothing. This isn't a contract, and you shouldn't feel that once you've discovered your guiding principle, you're committed for life. Your guiding principle will be a reflection of who you are and how you understand yourself right now—it makes a fantastic goal to aim for and will lead you to success. But finding and pursuing it shouldn't be a chore.

THE "SMALL SATISFACTIONS" WAY TO FIND YOUR GUIDING PRINCIPLE

So just what does a guiding principle look like? We'll show you. But first, know that its true meaning is only fully known by the person who owns it. If the examples we give below seem vague, that's because they are not yours, and you don't understand what the person means by the words used. But when you find your own, it will be crystal clear.

A Field Guide to Guiding Principles

- "I Am an Admired Creator of Concepts." (This is the person who might want to write a critically acclaimed book, or invent the next generation of widgets, to the accolades of her peers.)

- "I Am a Helpful Constructor of Structures." (Some sort of Habitat for Humanity business sounds ideal.)

- "I Playfully Teach Computers." (How about starting a fun/funny computer class or video instruction manual?)

They look innocuous enough. But when you find the one that rings your bell it will give you the kind of direction, determination, and passion that will turn you into a supercharged version of your former self (well, it'll be pretty helpful).

Trivial Pursuit

Although we don't want to turn this book into a cheap therapy session, we're going to have to delve deeply into your childhood. Brace yourself.

The idea here is that the indications of your guiding principle are scattered about in your personal history. Even though you may have been an obnoxious brat or conformist snob to all outward appearances, your inner guiding principle has emerged in your life through all its stages. The trick is to find its tracks.

First, make a list. List all those little, frivolous things you've done that gave you a real sense of satisfaction. Nothing important on this list, please: just the insignificant stuff.

Why restrict yourself to trivia? There are two reasons:

1. Many of our impressive, important accomplishments were done for or with the noisy approval of others. How can you be sure if becoming the first six-year-old to play the cello with the London Philharmonic Orchestra was something you found truly satisfying? Maybe it was just something that got you gobs of recognition, approval, and candy.

2. If important accomplishments are allowed, people tend to fixate on trying to remember them: "I'm sure I've done *something* significant in the past twenty-six years. If only I could recall what it was." Then they get depressed, manic, or inventive instead of just doing the exercise.

So insignificance and satisfaction are the most important keys to this exercise. A secondary guideline is that you focus only on those things *you did*. "Found a Captain Midnight Decoder Ring in a dumpster" is insignificant enough, and definitely satisfying enough, but what did you really do to get there? "Went dumpster-diving every weekend for six months and found some neat stuff, including a decoder ring" is better—it's something you did. Know that stuff you did is more telling—we don't want your guiding principle to be "I am a lucky stumbler-upon of silly things."

You'll end up with a list something like this:

- Made a really cool-looking sculpture of a lizard in high school art class (but it blew up in the kiln—true story).

- Learned how to do long division before anyone else in math class and got a gold star.

- Floss every day.

- Made upwards of ten dollars a day selling nightcrawlers to fisherfolk when I was seven.

- Told my mother not to buy me shirts with little rhinestone buttons on them.

- Covered my face with tattoos.

- Learned to juggle chainsaws.

- Bellydanced proficiently—and was subject of feature article in the *Bellydance Bugle*.

- Became a vegetarian.

- Learned how to ride a motorcycle.

But your list will be much, much longer. Aim for about twenty small satisfactions. Remember to include examples from all the different phases of your life. You might find it easier to break up your life by school grades. Dig out four memories each from:

- elementary school

- junior high

- high school

- college, and

- whenever.

You can also try this exercise by age, dividing your life up into quarters and then adding a free-for-all fifth category. Or just disregard chronology altogether and list satisfactions as they occur to you.

Here are some questions that can help you remember small satisfactions:

- Think of the best friends you had at various times. What did you do with them that was most fun? What made you proud?

- Can you remember a time when you got really pissed off because you weren't getting the recognition you deserved? Did this ever happen for some petty little reason? What did you do that deserved recognition?

- Was there something you were afraid to do at first but now look back on fondly or do regularly?

- Think of something that you used to enjoy that you're now embarrassed about (For example, you played *Dungeons and Dragons,* spent hours dressing and undressing Barbie, or dressed up for *The Rocky Horror Picture Show*). Is it something that gave you much satisfaction before you learned how uncool it was?

- What did you spend a lot of time doing? Maybe it was something that you wanted to keep doing after your friends got bored. Or maybe you spent so much time doing it that you didn't have any friends.

- What was something you enjoyed that you stopped doing because you realized that you weren't very good at it? (Probably thanks to some helpful person who told you.)

One more thing before you start your list: As you write down each memory, explain briefly why it gave you satisfaction, why it made you proud. Be as exact as possible—the details are important. So:

"Made a lizard in high school art class" becomes...

Sculpted a lizard out of clay in high school art class. Everyone else made cats, but I did my own thing, and went to the library to find pictures of a lizard so I'd get it right. I had to figure out how the muscles were attached to make the legs look real. It turned out really well, and it was a big surprise: no one expected that I had any artistic talent. The most satisfying things were how unexpected it was, how good it turned out (before it blew up in the kiln), and how much I enjoyed working the clay.

And "learned to ride a motorcycle" becomes...

Went to a class to learn how to ride a motorcycle (which is a pretty weenie way to learn). But learned to ride better than most people who just hop on and ride—learned about controlling a skid, using the clutch to stabilize the bike. The most satisfying thing is just riding around...the speed and freedom and *ow!* how cool I look. And the feeling that I'm putting one over on everybody: Who'd believe that I, Cecil Earthworm III would ever be tooling around on a Harley?

Sometimes, as in this example, you'll find yourself being judgmental ("...a pretty weenie way to..."). That's not a bad sign—you ought to pay extra attention to what it is you're judging, because that's a clue that you are closing in on something pretty hot. Saying that going to class is a weenie way to learn to ride a bike probably means that Cecil is either pretty attached to learning or to being seen as cool. Either way, this is good information for him—he shouldn't start a doily factory if he's concerned with being cool, and he shouldn't try to become a computer consultant without taking classes, if that's his preferred way of learning.

Now *write*. Right now, write.

Done? Of course you are. (If you're not, stop here, and do the writing.)

Checks and Balances: Extracting Your Guiding Principle

Once you have a list of your small satisfactions, complete with explanations, you can extract your guiding principle.

You'll do this in three stages, focusing on the following components of your guiding principle:

- Qualities. What you want to be: funny, helpful, admired, innovative, etc.

- Actions. What you want to do: evaluate, perform, plan, influence, etc.

- Subjects. What you want to work with: animals, programs, theories, art, etc.

The extraction process is simple, even if it does sound painful. You just look over what you wrote and compare it to the lists below. Every time there's something in the list that you have in your small satisfaction description, put a check mark next to it in the charts below.

The categories don't have to match exactly—think of them as general headings. And if you aren't sure which one to check, make a judgment. As long as you are reasonably consistent and as long as *you* know what you mean, everything works fine.

Qualities

The first thing to do is focus on how you want to be—the quality that you associate with satisfaction. Although this often does not determine the *type* of activity you'll choose to do, it is critical to discovering the *style* that will be most satisfying to you.

Now go through the list of small satisfactions you just made and notice all the qualities you mentioned—the ways you describe yourself and other people would describe you that give you satisfaction.

In the motorcycle example above, Cecil mentioned being "better than most people," "how cool I look," and the "feeling that I'm putting one over on everybody." As Cecil goes through each of his small satisfactions descriptions, he'll put a check mark next to the category in the list below each time he mentions something that fits. Only Cecil really knows exactly what he found satisfying about "putting one over on everybody," or what he means by "cool." That's fine. He's doing this for himself.

He might check "The best" or "Smart" for being "better than most" and "Individualistic" for "putting one over on people." If he feels that his sense of satisfaction comes from both categories, he should check both. Or if he finds that "putting one over" comes up a lot, maybe he'll start a category called "Defying Expectations."

So just check the category (or categories) you think most appropriate. Because there's a near-infinite number of possible motivating qualities (unlike Actions or Subjects), you may have to make your own categories. Feel free. The only limitation is that it comes from your small satisfactions descriptions, and that it fits into this form: *I am satisfied when I am, or when other people see me as...*

Qualities Checklist			
Unique/Individualistic		Famous/Notorious	
Powerful/In control		Respected/Admired	
The best		Helpful/Generous	
Efficient/Effective		Smart/Insightful	
Creative/Intuitive		Decisive	
Authentic		Tolerant/Open-minded	
Resourceful		Playful/Funny	
Honest/Candid		Loyal	
Diplomatic/Tactful		Patient	
Persistent/Driven/Focused		Curious/Enthusiastic	
Courageous/Brave		Empathetic/Understanding	

Now count your check marks. There is probably a cluster of categories that have most of the check marks (probably three or four, but could be more or less). Write the categories in the cluster in the Qualities Cluster column on page 13. Now it's time to examine your Actions.

Actions

Go through your list and look for all the verbs you wrote down. What you're actually doing is extracting the actions that gave you satisfaction—so make allowances for vocabulary and grammar. Make a check mark next to the category in the Actions Checklist each time you have an action that belongs in it.

Harley-riding Cecil would put one check next to "Learned" (even though he used the word three times, it refers to one event) and "Implemented" (because he put what he learned into practice by "riding" and "tooling around").

Do this for each of your small satisfaction descriptions. Again, there's some subjectivity in this process. But a little subjectivity is a good thing—you're the subject, after all.

So if you don't know where something should be grouped, do whatever feels right. It is. If you think that your "researched" should be in "Organized" instead of "Learned," put it there. If you decide that "researched" is both "Learning" *and* "Organizing," put a check next to both categories.

If you come up with actions for which we have no categories, create your own. But the list is fairly exhaustive. If you find yourself creating many new categories, you may just want to check "Developed."

Here's the list. Check away.

Actions Checklist			
	Constructed/Made		Learned/Researched
	Counseled/Advised		Managed/Administered
	Created/Innovated		Organized/Synthesized
	Developed/Improved		Performed/Demonstrated
	Evaluated/Analyzed		Planned/Strategized
	Formulated/Theorized		Shared/Helped
	Implemented/Did		Supervised/Directed
	Influenced/Convinced		Taught/Explained
	Investigated/Experimented		Visualized/Conceptualized

Here are two rules that may very well be of assistance if you get confused. Rule One: If you are not sure whether you can really tell the difference between two categories, check whichever feels right. This exercise has a lot more to do with what feels right than any rigid set of guidelines. Rule Two: If you want to check two categories for one activity, go ahead. In case you hadn't noticed by now, we just love making rules.

When you're done checking off these items, find the cluster of most-often checked Actions and put them in the Actions Cluster column, on page 13.

Subjects

Okay, this exercise should have given you a better sense of what it is you really like to do. And now that you know what you like to do, you have to figure out what you like to do it *to*. That's right, you're looking for the objects of your desires now, the nouns that you verb. You know the drill—put a check mark next to each one that you find in your written description.

Subjects Checklist			
	Animals		Art/Design/Music
	Concepts/Ideas		Details/Data
	Hardware/Equipment/Computers		Language/Symbols
	Mechanical Things		Money/Profits
	Needs/Causes		People/Relationships
	Physical Materials		Plants
	Policy/Strategy		Principles/Values
	Projects/Programs		Structural Things
	Systems/Methods		Theories/Formulae

Now transfer the cluster of most-often checked subjects into the Subjects Cluster column on page 13.

The Guiding Principle Clusters

	Qualities Cluster	Actions Cluster	Subjects Cluster
1			
2			
3			
4			
5			
6			

Now you have three short lists—one for each cluster of qualities, actions, and subjects. Don't worry if you don't have the same number of categories in each cluster—it's just a coincidence if you do.

Mix 'n' Match

It's time to find the one sentence that sums up your guiding principle. You've got a list of the things that give you the most satisfaction, that make you proud. From these you'll extract the principle that will be the foundation upon which you'll build a successful, fulfilling business. Here's how to do it:

Play with the possible permutations of this sentence: I am a (Quality) (Action) of (Subject).

Your sentences probably won't make any grammatical sense: "I am a Funny Developed of Plans," for example. So consider the sentence structure a starting point. You may want to change your qualities into adjectives: "I Humorously Develop Plans." Or change your actions into nouns: "I am a Funny Developer of Plans." Hell, we don't care. Change your quality into a coordinating pluperfect subjunctive if you want, as long as you use your own language to say what you really mean.

And play with the words themselves as well as the structure of the sentence. So if you have "I Helpfully Influence People," you may want to make it a bit more specific: "I am a supportive coach for families." But you don't want to get too specific: "I actively listen and sympathetically respond to single-mother families living in South Boise while advising them about healthy nutritional decision-making." That might contain the seed of a great business, so keep it around, but it is not a guiding principle—those are more general.

Start connecting the phrases in the three columns in as many combinations as you can find. Think about what they mean, why each one is on your list. Play with all the possibilities. Some of them won't make much sense. There are many possible combinations—if you have just four in each category, there are sixty-four possibilities. Don't feel that you have to identify and weigh each one. Just let your eyes wander and your mind make connections, and see what happens.

There's no rigid technique. You're just waiting for something to click. When you get a sentence that's intriguing, electrifying, or just extra-neat, write it down. If they all seem intriguing, only write down the electrifying ones. If they seem, at best, barely adequate, write down the barely adequate ones (and get a cup of coffee).

When you're done combining, look at what you've written and pick out the one that clicks loudest, the one that sets your heart beating a bit faster. It might not be the one you're most comfortable with. You may immediately think "This is stupid, I can never do that, I haven't the money or the experience, or..." The more you react to one of these, *even if the reaction is defensive or negative,* the more likely it's truly important to you. (And, by the way, you may be right about not having the money, experience, or whatever, to achieve your purpose *right now*. But it will make your life a whole lot more exciting if you at least aim in the right direction, even if you can barely see the target at the moment.)

If you're having a tough time deciding which possible guiding principle really floats your boat, answer these questions:

- If I had to dedicate myself to aiming for one of these goals for three years, and I knew I wouldn't get the reactions from other people that I really want, which would I do?

- If someone offered me a fortune to give up using all the abilities in these sentences, which one would I not give up? (What is it you cannot help but do because it's just the way you are?)

- If you met a bunch of people, each of whom embodied one of your sentences, who would you most envy? Who would you want to mentor you? Whose "right-hand person" would you want to be?

If you're still not completely satisfied, look at your top two or three choices. Then pick one that just might be your favorite. You're not making any commitment, understand, just indicating that it sounds pretty good. Have you picked the phrase that comes closest to expressing your guiding principle, even though you're not willing to be totally committed to it? Good.

We lied—you just made a commitment. That *is* your purpose for the next year. We don't care if you're feeling wishy-washy about it— that's it, you're done, finished, complete. Write it down, put it in your wallet, tape it to your mirror, hum it under your breath—it's better to decide on something that's not completely perfect than to sit around with your thumb up your...nose waiting for inspiration. You've got a perfectly good guiding principle, made up of components you find satisfying, that comes as close as possible to expressing your purpose. Even if it's not perfect, it will serve you well if you let it.

But what about all those other Qualities, Actions, and Subjects that are important to you, but didn't make the final cut? We'll just call those your preferences—they're not absolutely essential, but are still very important. The more of them you incorporate into your business, the happier you'll be. So keep them in mind when you're messing about with your guiding principle in the next couple of chapters. You may find yourself substituting one of your preferences for a part of your guiding principle, and you can imagine how we feel about that: it's your life, and you should do whatever makes sense to you.

Discovering Your
Hidden Resources

YOU MIGHT BE SURPRISED to discover that, probably despite yourself, you've amassed a fairly impressive number of resources. Your credit cards may be maxed out, your job may require that you wear a hairnet, and you may live in the unconverted basement of a sweatshop—but there are resources to be found nonetheless.

But isn't money the only resource that really matters? Not hardly. In fact, there's a school of small-business startup thought that says too much money can be as great a problem as too little. It's possible—and not uncommon—for startup companies to spend a tremendous amount of money without spending a cent on anything that will make a sale. You don't have that luxury. Your business will start tiny, and you'll use your ingenuity, determination, and guiding principle to develop its fundamental strengths. You'll become obsessed with feedback and customer satisfaction, because you have to be. In the end, you'll have a lean, mean, fightin'-machine of a business.

So there's no possible way for you to form a dysfunctional dependence on money, simply because you don't have any. Instead, you *must* grow your business with whatever fertilizer you can find.

MAPPING YOUR RESOURCES

There are two ways to uncover your resources. One is to make lists. List all the people and skills you know and all the stuff you have. But lists can be uninspiring, and it's easy to overlook some important resources, or to not dig deeply enough into the ones that you do list. So the other option is to use the mind map.

We chose mind mapping for a very simple reason: because it works. Once you get past the initial "Why am I making silly diagrams instead of an organized outline?" reaction, you'll find that ideas come easily and completely, information is organized in a natural way, and you make intuitive associations and leaps. Plus it's good clean fun. Even if you think all you've done with your life is convert oxygen to carbon dioxide, you will have incidentally accumulated enough resources to nurture and guide your budding multinational corporation. The resources in question are:

- your stuff,

- your skills and areas of knowledge, and

- your contacts (the people you can impose upon).

After you uncover as many of your resources as you can, you'll combine them with your guiding principle and the path to business success will open before you.

Here is the basic mind-mapping process: Write the main concept (which will be your stuff, skills, or people) in a circle in the middle of a blank page. Draw a line radiating from the central concept to whatever you associate with it. Then make associations to those things, and so on. Well, it's easier to understand than to explain. Look at the pictures. Then do what you see.

The creators of mind mapping use colors and pictures in their maps. (And, in fact, they might not recognize our abridged mind mapping technique as genuine. If you want the full benefits of mind mapping, check out the books in the Resources section at the end of this book.) But don't worry if your maps are messy. Just try to make them as complete as possible given that you're focusing on resources that are useful or unusual. If you try to map absolutely everything, you'll be halfway done next month. Instead, focus on whatever is potentially useful or unusual.

For example, when mapping your stuff, you don't have to make an inventory of everything you own. Just try to include everything useful or unusual. So include your useful car. Include your unusual collection of velvet Elvises. Don't bother including your spatula (unless it's part of a useful, complete kitchen set or is an unusual, Elvis-shaped spatula).

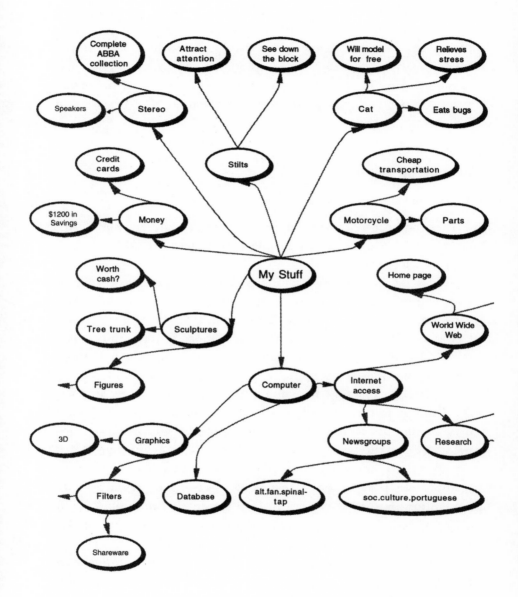

YOUR STUFF MAP

The first map you'll make is a map of your possessions. Don't panic—this isn't the most important list. Write "My Stuff" in the middle of the page and circle it. Now draw lines to short descriptions of stuff you have.

Although we'll say again that money is not the most important of your resources, it is stuff. Include it here (and don't forget credit).

If you're having trouble recalling all of your useful or unusual stuff, you might want to use the following questions to jog your memory:

- Do you have any hobbies, or abandoned hobbies, for which you bought stuff?

- Do you have any stuff you've never been able to part with, for no apparent reason?

- Do you have stuff you trot out on special occasions, to amuse, horrify, or intrigue guests?

- Do you have anything that you're constantly lending to friends?

- Do you have anything that strangers comment on? How about anything *other* than body-piercings, tattoos, or attitude?

Try to rack your brain until you have at least a half-dozen lines leading to your stuff. If you've only got three or four, don't worry. It may be depressing, but it's not going to ruin you for business. If you've got absolutely nothing, make a list (or mind map) of all the useful or unusual free things you can get your hands on. Snails, weeds, cardboard boxes, old tires, whatever. If it's free and strikes you as useful or unusual, write it down.

OK. Now you've got an incipient mind map, consisting of "My Stuff" in the middle surrounded by a bunch of descriptions of your actual stuff in circles. Now look at each thing and map the features it has and the benefits it offers. Benefits, as opposed to features, *are things your stuff can do for you*, not just things they can do. The fact that a printer prints at a super-speedy eight pages per minute is a feature. The fact that it saves you time makes this a benefit.

With some things, you won't be able to think of many features/benefits. That's fine. For others, you may go wild. That's even better. Eventually, you'll end up with a mind map that looks something like the one on page 18.

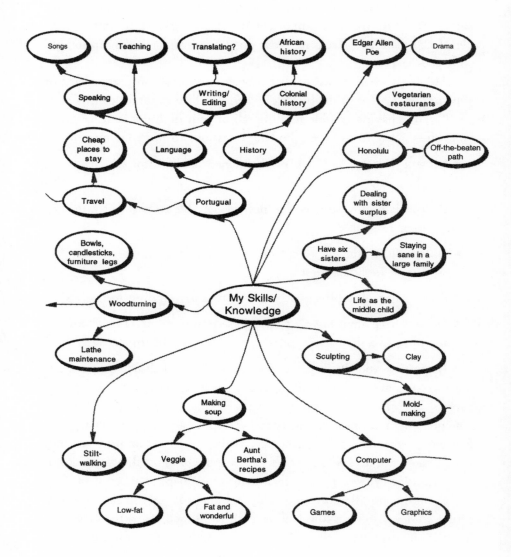

Your Skills/Knowledge Map

The second map you'll be doing is the Skills/Knowledge Map. After you write "My Skills/Knowledge" in the central circle, you want to start mapping your skills. Skills are self-explanatory. List everything you can do fairly well—typing, playing bass, training your dog, bicycling, writing naughty limericks, shopping for shoes, fixing toilets, whatever—and that you find at least marginally interesting. Include whatever you can do with the stuff from your "My Stuff" map, and skills you've learned in classes, from hobbies, and on the job.

After you finish with your skills, start with your areas of knowledge. This is a bit less straightforward. Include things you know about (the mating habits of the blowfish, how ambulance services operate), and things you are (left-handed, alcoholic, bald, libertarian). Here the big questions are: What do you know? What are you?

Remember research you've done, odd infatuations you've had, trends you've followed. If you know everything about the Brady Bunch, include that. If you've followed Ringo Starr's career with great interest, include that. Include whatever knowledge you think is fascinating or functional.

Then include knowledge based on who and what you are—gay, Nebraskan, post-modern, allergic to grass, etc. Focus on those characteristics that set you apart from the majority.

Then make associations to all the skills and areas of knowledge you just mapped. An example is on page 20. Extend the map as many levels as you want. "Fixing toilets" may become "plumbing," or it may become "fixing the toilets in the dorms at college." If it becomes "plumbing," that may lead you to map the rest of your plumbing skills. If it becomes "fixing the toilets in the dorms," that may lead you to map all your other dorm repair skills. Play with this until you've done a fairly comprehensive job of mapping your most interesting skills and areas of knowledge.

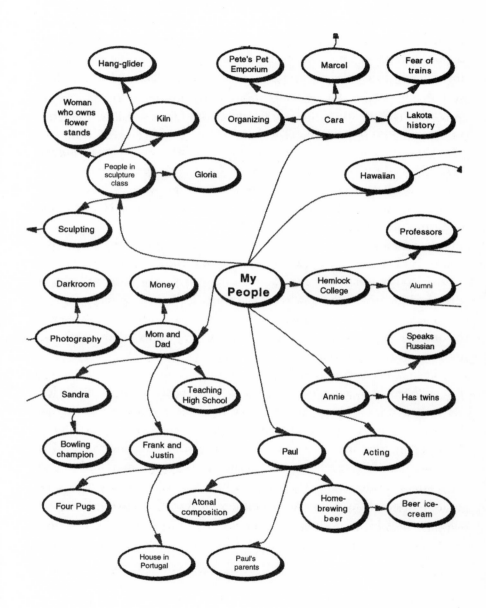

YOUR PEOPLE MAP

You could spend several days making your People Map. We'll give you the brief overview, in case you're as lazy as we are. If you want to get more out of this exercise, get yourself some BIG pieces of paper and go into minute detail.

The central circle says, of course, "My People." Include in the first level all the people you are comfortable imposing upon. Try to dredge up people from as many different facets of your life as possible. Remember to include family (immediate and distant), friends from different periods of your life, classmates, teammates, people in group therapy with you, and teachers or mentors.

Also include groups and organizations to which you belong. For example, if you're Jewish, and are willing to impose upon the Jewish community to some degree, that should be in your map. If you're a member of Earth First! and are willing to ask them if you can license their name for your line of tree spikes, put them on your list.

At this point you've completed the first level of your People Map. Now look at each person and group and map *their* resources. That's right, map the Stuff, Skills/Knowledge, and People to which they have access. We've provided an example on page 22. (Yes, this exercise *could* go on forever.) Don't even try to make these maps complete, though. The better you know your people, the more of their resources you'll be able to map. That's appropriate. But unless you have a week to spare, focus on resources that you're willing to use. If a friend of a friend has a great resource, but you're not willing to ask if you can borrow it, it's not a great resource.

Now you have three maps: one of your stuff and the benefits of your stuff, one of your skills/areas of knowledge, and one of the people you know and their resources. We're willing to bet that you got tired of mapping before you ran out of things to map. But if you still feel that you have a pitiful number of resources, consider the following:

- Did you squeeze all the possible benefits from your possessions?

- Did you extend your skills map as far as you could? Did you reduce skills to their smallest components and map those? Did you enlarge skills as much as possible to find other skills in the same category?

- Did you examine all parts of your life for areas of knowledge? These don't have to be the "authorized" fields that are taught in school. You might have learned something by growing up in your crazy family or having to move often, by living with a psychotic housemate, or by dating a married person. And you don't have to know everything about it—just more than most.

- Did you get out a ream of paper and try mapping each of your people individually? Did you treat them to the same scrutiny you imposed upon yourself?

If you do all of the above, you'll find that you have an amazing array of raw resources. The challenge is to combine them to discover your perfect business.

How? The answers are in chapter 3.

Developing an Outline
of Your Ideal Business

YOUR **IDEAL BUSINESS** would incorporate your whole guiding principle and wouldn't require more than your existing resources. You would be performing your favorite action on your favorite things (concepts, knowledge, whatever), and you'd have easy access to those things. Simple enough. But how do you get from here to there? How do you get from "I'm a resourceful developer of structures" to an actual business?

Well, first you generate ideas that combine your action and your subject with your resources. Then you focus those ideas, add customers, and *voilà!*—a viable small business.

The ideas you'll be generating are quick sweeps of the business opportunity brush: ideas such as designing motorcycle paraphernalia or teaching cat care. They usually won't be practical businesses per se, but they will often contain the kernel of a worthwhile business idea or, at least, point in a profitable direction.

After you've established a number of these business areas, you'll look through the Business Idea Directory in chapter 4 to find ideas that match what you're looking for, spark a related idea, or fuse with your main ideas to provide extra oomph. Or you can ignore the Idea Directory and develop your own ideas from nothing more than the products of your mind (and your guiding principle and resources, of course).

THE RESOURCE PRINCIPLE

In the resources column in the chart below, write down all your resources that are even remotely related to your subject. If your subject is "Animals," go through your mind maps looking for animals or any-thing related to animals. If you liked the subject enough for it to appear in your guiding principles cluster, it's almost certain that you'll have resources in that area. But they may not jump out at you. Remember to include not only your actual animal companions but anything that's *related* to animals: your knowledge of the proper diet for lizards; your skill at cleaning fish tanks; your Uncle Ernie's parakeet that whistles songs from *Les Miserables;* your friend who grew up on a chicken ranch; the beekeeping class you took in college.

Resources related to Subject: Animals	**Action:** *Teaching* turns resources into....
Knowledge of beekeeping	Teach how to be a beekeeper/how to be a better beekeeper.
	Teach how bees improve crops. (Teach farmers?)
	Teach about insect societies.
Aquarium cleaning/maint. skills	Teach how to clean aquariums.
Cat that poops in the toilet	Offer cat potty training services.
	Teach people how to toilet-train their cats (in person, through books, videotape).
Uncle Ernie's singing parakeet	Teach music or music appreciation, using the bird as a prop.
	Teach about oddities of animal behavior.
	Train and sell "prerecorded" parakeets— singing Beethoven, opera, Japanese flute music, pop songs.
Am vegetarian	Teach how to cook vegetarian meals, or how to raise vegetarian kids or pets.
Knowledge of proper lizard diet	Teach lizard care and feeding.
	Teach how to breed or make lizard food (specialized per lizard species/age/sex. Through a booklet or kit?)
	Organize teaching tours to see the Komodo dragons feed.
Friend's mom is a vet	Teach people how they can tell when to take their animal to the vet, what they can do at home.

Unless you're having a hard time listing subject-related resources, don't try to force a connection. Just focus on the resources in which you're most interested and that relate most easily to your subject.

When you're done with your resources it's time to start looking for some action. For each resource listed, ask: "What can my action do with this?" If your guiding principle is "I'm a generous *teacher* of animals," then you're asking, "What can teaching do with my knowledge of lizard diets?" We're still brainstorming here, so don't judge your ideas—just get them down on paper. Your goal is not to have a perfect business idea pop full-blown out of your head, but to start focusing on potential areas that would be fun and fulfilling.

Now do it. Using the chart below, write down all your subject-related resources.

Resources related to Subject:	Action: turns resources into....

Now plug in your action and brainstorm. What can your action do to your resources? Go wild. If no terrific ideas come hopping out of your subconscious, don't worry. Of course, if you do have any terrific ideas for specific businesses, write them down. But don't spend too much time on them. The business directory that follows this chapter is chock-full o' ideas, and will help get your juices flowing.

In any case, jot down as many combinations of your subject-related resources and actions as you can.

Now that you're done, you might think that many of the results of this exercise are too narrow (or ridiculous) to be feasible. You might be right. But don't worry. If you found nothing obviously practical as a result of this exercise, that's fine. You'll work on the viability of your business ideas later.

Neither of us is an animal teacher. But we still came up with some ideas which, even if they're goofy, point in the direction of possible business areas. If you love animals and you love teaching, organizing a business around the above will provide truly satisfying work. And even if what you end up doing isn't an exact match to your guiding principle—if you're leading wildlife tours, you'll probably feel more like a tour guide than a teacher-about-animals—there will be a core of guiding principle there to energize, interest, and reward you.

The Business
Idea Directory

YOU'VE DISCOVERED YOUR GUIDING PRINCIPLE, you've uncovered your resources, and you've found where they overlap in possible business areas. You are amazing. But what you haven't done is any hard-headed, customer-centered, money-oriented business strategizing. We'll be easing into that slooooowly, starting with this section—the Business Idea Directory.

When you see an idea that matches one of your possible business areas, or fits your action or subject, make a note of it. And when you see an idea that is not related to anything you've done in this book but interests you nonetheless, mark that too.

This isn't meant to be an exhaustive list of possible businesses. Since the right business for you will probably be unique, an exhaustive list is impossible. But there are people running all of the following businesses successfully, either full- or part-time. This section will give you an idea of the scope of possible businesses, provide you with basic, ready-to-customize business templates, and help you refine the results of the brainstorming you did in the last chapter.

A note about business opportunity packages: A business opportunity package is basically a watered-down franchise. You get a plan explaining how to run your business, a support line to call, contacts with suppliers, and the sense that what you're doing is possible. And, while they're by no means as extensive as franchises, business opportunities don't charge a royalty—just a one-time fee. They can offer an easier way to start a business.

But there are major problems with business opportunity packages: they are usually overpriced, overhyped, and unsatisfying. If you can find one that is reasonably priced, with very convincing figures to back up statements of possible income, and hooked up to your guiding principle, go for it. But go for it after you've called *all* their current business owners. Get the names of all their buyers for the past few years and call as many as you can stand. And before you buy, ask yourself the big question—can I start this business on my own, without the business opportunity package? Look in *Entrepreneur Magazine,* which has an annual directory of business opportunities, or the quarterly *Business Opportunities Handbook* for listings of business opportunity packages.

Multilevel marketing (MLM) organizations offer similar opportunities. Although the best-known of these MLMs are Mary Kay and

Amway, there are now MLMs selling virtually every kind of product. You earn money in MLMs by selling a product directly and by receiving a percentage of the income of other salespeople you recruit. If you're interested in an MLM, do three things: stay away from "get-rich-quick" plans, stay away from MLMs that emphasize recruiting instead of selling product, and plan on working steadily at the business for a substantial length of time before you see a substantial amount of money. But if you can find a product or service you believe in, an MLM can become profitable, especially as an add-on to another business.

The following "directory" is divided into thirteen chapters: animals, art, business, computers, crafts, data and figures, domestic, eco-friendly, health, music, farming and plants, writing and language, and miscellaneous.

We've included the briefest possible descriptions. If you find a business you're interested in, you can get more information from your library or bookstore. Or, if that doesn't work, check out the *Encyclopedia of Associations* and *Newsletters in Print* in the library. Virtually every group has its own association or newsletter that will be able to point you in the right direction. If all else fails, call someone who's already doing the business in another location and ask them for advice.

Happy hunting!

chapter four

Animals

MONEY MAY NOT BE ABLE to buy you love, but love just might be able to make you some money. If you love animals—from predatory wasps to fuzzy bunnies—check out the following sixteen business ideas.

Aquarium Cleaning/Maintenance/Set-up

Most aquarium owners—both offices and individuals—dread cleaning the tank scum. If you don't, and can do the job thoroughly and quickly, you can make a good income from a fairly modest number of steady customers. Also look into supplying (by re-selling, breeding, growing, or manufacturing) the aquariums with fish, invertebrates, plants, or those cute little castles. You can also offer set-up services, mostly to businesses that are opening new offices or redecorating.

Animal Breeder

Specialize in one breed or an exotic animal type for which there's some demand and almost no supply. Because you're dealing with living things, you must understand how to keep the animals healthy and happy. This is especially true if you're breeding dogs, cats, birds, llamas, potbellied pigs, goat, ponies, rabbits, or exotic birds. It's probably less true if you're breeding worms or crickets (not to say that worms should be unhappy). If you breed a trainable animal, think about combining this business with being an animal trainer (see below).

Animal Groomer

Specialize by animal type: dogs, cats, horses, and so on. If you can offer unusual services such as house calls or the use of non-toxic materials, it'll be that much easier to carve out a niche for yourself.

Animal Sitter

Offer an alternative to kennels. You can bathe, feed, and exercise animals while their owners are away. Most pet owners would rather leave their pets at home in the loving care of a responsible (and probably bonded and insured) person instead of in the most comfortable kennel. Also offer the related house- and plant-sitting services.

Animal Trainer

If you're great with animals—or one specific kind of animal—you can become a trainer. The largest market is for dogs, such as puppy training, potty training, and barking and biting training. But there's a substantial market for horse trainers as well. And if you can train a cat, you'll have no problem finding clients who will pay dearly to have their aloof kitty come when they call.

Animal Exerciser

It's tough to make a full-time living as an animal exerciser. (Actually, all we can think of here is dog-walking, but we didn't want to limit your creativity—maybe you can play with cats or pet monkeys or something.) But it is a natural add-on for any of the other animal businesses listed—you can build your client list for your primary service while you walk.

Animal Products Retailer

Although you won't be working directly with animals, there are plenty of opportunities to make money selling animal-related merchandise. From custom-made doghouses or birdhouses to horse blankets to cat toys, people love to pamper their pets and will pay for the chance. Or you can sell animal-related products for people—kitten-shaped soapdishes and horse head candlesticks, for example.

Beekeeper

If parthenogenesis, royal jelly, and verroa mites are household words to you, you can become a commercial beekeeper. In addition to the bees, hives, and extracting equipment, you need good hive placement (contact farmers about a mutually beneficial arrangement). Don't overlook the non-honey products of the hive—beeswax, royal jelly, and bee pollen all sell to specialized markets for a healthy price.

Breed Beneficial Bugs

As more farms become organic, more farmers are searching for non-toxic ways to deal with pests. The best weapons of non-toxic pest control are bugs: ladybugs, lacewings, wasps (such as trichogramma and encarsia formosa), and beneficial nematodes (microscopic organisms, sold in paste form, that eat the nasty nematodes in the soil). Worms are also valuable to farmers and gardeners, and worm farming can provide a full-time living.

Doggie Day Care

We didn't make this up. You drive your van around to your clients' houses in the morning and collect their dogs. You bring the dogs to your doggie place and let them socialize, supervising them all the while. You can also offer grooming services, playtime with a human, and can give the dogs any medication they need.

Horse Services

With the right skills, knowledge, and connections, you can start a horse care and exercising, shoeing, or riding instruction business. Combine these businesses to offer a full-service, one-stop horse business.

Pet Transportation

Transport pets to the veterinarian or kennel while their owners are working or otherwise unavailable, or to the beach or other pet-friendly locations for special walks. If you've got the vehicle, horse transportation is another possibility. This business may not be able to stand on its own, so combine it with another animal business for the best results.

Pet Alternative Healer

Although you don't want to tread on the domain of the vet, you can offer alternative health services for pets. Cleanse their auras, give them paw reflexology, massage them, feed them blue-green algae. If you've got the touch, you can comfort animals and owners and build a solid business on referrals. Don't scoff—Linda Tellington-Jones, whose "TTouch" infomercials you may have seen on TV, has developed an extensive empire out of this business idea.

Pet Cemetery Owner

Well, it's depressing. But if you've got access to land...

Pet ID Services/Pet Detective

You can help recover stolen or lost pets by starting a pet registry containing photos and identifying information. If a pet goes missing, you search information at the Humane Society, animal shelters, police department, and classified ads. You can also work with a vet and offer electronic ID services.

Pet Food Manufacturer

Would *you* eat that rank-smelling stuff you feed your pet? Nothing in that foul ooze can be what the doctor ordered, so if you can develop a recipe for healthful, tasty pet food and cook it up in batches, you can sell it to local pet owners. Maybe you can even deliver a weekly supply to their homes. Remember to emphasize the benefits: longer life, a prettier coat, a happier animal.

Art

YOU MAY NOT KNOW MUCH ABOUT BUSINESS, but you know what you like: art. Of course, some art-related businesses do require talent, or at least a modicum of technical ability, but there are plenty of opportunities out there for art lovers who couldn't draw a straight line with a ruler and a drafting table. Whichever category you're in, one of the following eighteen business possibilities may suit you to a T-square.

ART GALLERIES

If being a market-be-damned fine artist is your passion, we have some good news: you *can* make money selling your art, no matter what your guidance counselor told you. Now the bad news: you'll have to base your business strategy on the fact that you aren't going to become an internationally renowned celebrity artist anytime soon. Sure, it'll happen eventually. Just not soon.

Instead of hustling to get into the hottest venues in New York and Paris, hustle to get your work into your local galleries. Attend events, network with other artists, promote galleries when they do show your work, and be all-around businesslike. Realize that there are many artists who never show in galleries and still make a living selling their fine art—galleries are not the only, or even necessarily the best, sales channel for you.

If you're as interested in getting into galleries as you are in actually selling your art, check your local library for books and talk with people to learn the best approaches.

Other Places to Get Hung

Selling through galleries alone is a fairly passive way to make money with your art. You don't have much control over getting shown or making sales. If you want to make more sales without becoming too commercial, other "acceptable" channels for exposing your art are:

Competitions

Exhibitions/Trade shows

Corporations

Retail Businesses (boutiques, bookstores, restaurants, etc.)

Upscale offices (chiropractors, architects, realtors, etc.)

Slide registries

Art reps

Interior designers

Churches/Synagogues/Mosques, etc.

Universities and colleges

Local museums

If you want to show your work in any of these venues, most books on fine art marketing will tell you who to contact and how to approach them. It is possible to make sales this way, especially if you're thoroughly professional.

You can follow in the footsteps of many great artists by creating some art for money and some art for love (and promoting the second category like crazy until it makes money too). Creating some of your art for money elevates you out of the ranks of the unemployable poseurs and into the ranks of the income-producing artists. It also expands your diet beyond six-for-a-dollar ramen noodles. This is good. If you want to be a balanced artistic mercenary, read on.

SPECIALIZED ART

Pick a niche. Let's say you noticed "Offices, Chiropractic" in the list above (though that list is anything but exhaustive). Can you do a series of "crooked spine" oils? How about a herniated disk sculpture? They don't have to be realistic. If you can do art that would be appropriate for offices and has a chiropractic theme, there's a good chance you could develop a solid product—say, selling limited edition prints at chiropractic conventions, in *Chiropractic Today* magazine, and so on. Think about specializing in theme *and* medium—if your sculpture features dolls, could you sell to doll or toy manufacturers or collectors?

Portraitist

Granted this works best if you're a representational artist. But try offering abstract portraits and you'll be the only one on your block doing so. You should be able to parlay the sheer weirdness into press coverage. (Whether you'll get any clients is another question.) You can specialize in portrait type: boudoir, family, baby, newlywed, newly-divorced, and so on. Who could resist a cubist portrait of their newborn?

Don't limit yourself to people, though. You can do your clients' houses, animals (there are enough crazy horse, cat, and dog people out there to support any number of artists), favorite landscapes or cityscapes, boats, anything. We've heard of one artist who draws people's homes. She goes door to door selling her services and charges between $350 and $600 per painting. She makes a sale at about every fifteenth house—and brings home more money than she would working as an office drone.

Sell Reproductions

This isn't a business opportunity per se, but it's a powerful way to multiply the possible outlets for your art. Have your art printed on cards, posters, mouse pads, calendars, T-shirts, greeting cards, or anything else your print shop can produce. (You can find a commercial printer who works with fine art by reading the ads in national art magazines.) Sell through mail order, craft shows, and retail stores. Again, it helps if you specialize. If you do computer art that is notably "computer-y," perhaps you can sell mouse pads, keyboard covers, screen savers, CD-ROM holders, and other computer-related products.

Muralist

Find an ugly or boring section of wall that's attached to a business or home. Find the owners of said wall and ask if they'd like a mural painted. They'll probably expect to work closely with you on the design (a process which will be annoying), but you can get a good-sized sum for a mural, and it's a great way to promote your other work.

Airbrush Artist/Cartoonist

In addition to all the strategies for other artists, if you're fast enough, you can make money as an airbrush artist or cartoonist by "performing" at shows, fairs, and other festive occasions. As an airbrush artist you can reproduce art from pictures onto T-shirts, or paint clothing, vehicles, and even fingernails. And a cartoonist can try to expand into the competitive world of gag writing for greeting cards and syndication.

Commercial Artist

There are art markets for book and magazine covers and interior illustrations, CD and cassette covers, paper products, brochures, packaging, and giftware. You can contact art publishers who sell to frame shops, print galleries, and interior decorators, among others. There's also a demand for catalog, fashion, medical, and technical illustration. Check out the annual *Artist's and Graphic Designer's Market* from Writer's Digest Books for more information on who's looking for what. We recommend that instead of creating a slew of art and then hoping to find a home for it, you research the market, discover what's needed, and then provide it.

Tattoo Artist

Tattoos have become about as mainstream as earrings, but it's a whole lot easier to find someone to pierce your ears with the minimum necessary skill than to find an excellent tattoo artist. Word of mouth works wonders in this business, and you can diversify by offering branding and scarification as well. You'll need a license to be a tattoo artist in most areas.

Ice Sculptor

OK, you may get sick of making swans. But if you don't mind sculpting in public (which will be the case unless you can afford a very large portable freezer) and having your art disappear in a matter of hours, ice sculpting can provide you a living. Your work will be with caterers, event planners, and hotels.

Decorative Painter

You can decorate unfinished, used, or plain furnishings, fabrics, housewares, doodads, or anything else that doesn't move too fast. Paint whimsical, interesting, or just plain attractive designs and resell your products for a healthy profit. Or you can offer a Home Decorating Service: there is a growing demand for faux finishes and trompe l'oeil. A variation of this business is being a Children's Room Painter and specializing in designing unique, fantastic children's rooms.

ART-RELATED JOBS

As promised, what follows is a listing of jobs for all those people who love art, but just can't do it well enough to make a living at it (or for artists who want to explore other options).

Art Teacher/Tutor

This is a traditional money-making business for artists. And it works. Focus your efforts by art or student type, or both. You may focus on sculpture or watercolor classes for women, or seniors, or children, or recovering alcoholics. You might try to find a good target market first, and then offer classes. For example, if there seems to be a surplus of birdwatchers in your area, offer a "Capture Your Favorite Birds in Watercolor" class. Or try specializing by art type—you could offer "Color Field Painting for the Absolute Beginner."

Art Counselor

Although you may need a license to practice art therapy, you can be an art counselor just by saying that's what you are. Focus on people who need the healing power of art (anything from people who are institutionalized to people who have low self-esteem) and develop projects and classes that are engaging, fun, and helpful.

Local Art Merchandiser

Contact a number of local artists whose work you enthusiastically enjoy. Have reproductions (of whatever type) made of their best work, and sell the reproductions through local retail stores. You may need to offer them a consignment arrangement. Emphasize that the art is local and limited-issue, and set up a vending-type relationship, where you show up and restock displays (and get your money) on a regular basis.

Artists' Representative

Most artists dream of having a rep. A rep who will deal with all the headaches of their burgeoning art empire. A rep who'll be on a first-name basis with all the gallery owners in New York and Paris. A rep who'll guarantee international fame and fortune. A rep entirely unlike you. But while you have to be completely honest about your lack of international connections and experience, you can do a whole lot of good for an artist. Do all those things they ought to do but don't: prepare portfolios, approach/follow up with galleries, shmooze, sell reproductions, assemble a mailing list, host events, do public relations. In exchange for all this, you get a commission, typically 20 to 25 percent, of whatever you sell. Contact an experienced rep or Volunteer Lawyers for the Arts (1 East 53rd Street, 6th Floor, NY, NY 10022, (212) 319-2787). They usually work with artists, not art reps, but will still be able to provide information about contracts, exclusive representations, and other legal questions. Artists' reps can work with fine artists, photographers, craftspeople, and all other types of visual artists.

Art School

Assemble a bunch of personable, articulate artists who are interested in teaching for several hours a week. Develop a bunch of targeted, attractive classes and then market them like mad. You can't operate an art school out of your dingy little apartment, so a startup can be expensive if you can't find good, cheap teaching space.

Gallery Owner

We've tried to stay away from retail businesses because they can cost a fortune to start and go belly-up with alarming regularity. But no listing of art-related businesses would be complete without the art gallery. If you want to lose less money than most galleries, specialize in something of local, tourist, or special interest: regional landscapes, nature, erotic, maritime, or horse art, for example. Or you can specialize by cost, that is, low cost. Most people are priced out of the original art market, so if you can start a gallery with low retail prices, you might just be able to stay afloat. Exploit the labor of art students and starving artists who need cash to support their $150 per week art supplies habits. Making your gallery a cooperative venture is another way to make it financially feasible to start, though not necessarily to operate.

Photographer

Art photography can be sold the same way as fine art. But if you're interested in making a business as a freelance photographer, here are some markets to keep in mind: audiovisual, educational publishing, fashion, magazines, newspapers (daily and weekly), publicity and promotion, real estate, stock photo agencies, television, weddings and other events, and yearbooks. And, of course, there's portrait photography: family, boudoir, pet, baby, and so on. Think of people who want photos taken but are too busy to do so themselves, such as new home owners who are overwhelmed with their moves and will pay for prints that showcase their new homes for their friends and families.

Video Production

In addition to videotaping weddings, performances, seminars, yearbooks, resumes, and sporting events, you can produce real estate videos, local access television commercials, insurance documentation, or promotional videos. You can also provide video editing, transfer, and duplication services.

Business

IF YOU WANT TO START A SMALL BUSINESS serving other small businesses, this is the section for you. You can consult, calculate, plan, manage, or buy for them. Here are seventeen business opportunities for making a living while minding other people's business.

Advertising Agency

Although this business evokes images of expensive office suites full of artificial people trying to sell words that mean nothing to people who don't care, what we're talking about is a whole different ball game. You'll offer the services of a hands-on marketing agency rather than those of an advertising agency, and you'll focus on small, too-busy-to-market businesses. Because advertising is often not the best marketing strategy, you'll work with clients to discover what is, and how to implement it. You'll be doing everything from writing press releases to setting up cross-promotions to hosting special events. For a good introduction to marketing you need look no further than the marketing section of this very book.

Market Research

You can offer market research services to startup businesses or businesses thinking of introducing a new product or service. It's your job to discover if anyone will want what they're selling. You have to be able to target the right niche, ask the right questions, and understand the responses. Although a background in statistics is helpful, the big companies who can afford a comprehensive, scientific survey won't hire you anyway. It's the itty bitty companies who can use your service for small-scale market research. The challenge is finding businesses before they open. Try taking how-to-start-a-business classes, placing an ad in the businesses-for-sale section of the local classifieds, and networking like crazy.

Association Management

There is an association, club, or organization for almost everything. Most of these are tiny and don't need more than one or two volunteers to keep the dues flowing in. But once an association needs more than part-time attention, you can step in with association management services. You will keep track of memberships and dues, develop flyers and newsletters, and brainstorm more services to offer members and new ways to increase membership. If you have a tough time finding an association on the cusp of becoming too large for volunteers, you might think about starting your own. Do you have contacts/knowledge/interest in a group that isn't currently served by an association? A variation on association management is fan club management. If you can find a celebrity who's becoming sufficiently well-known to need someone to answer mail and organize a newsletter, you can make your money as a professional sycophant, er, fan club manager.

Bartering Service

Small businesses need each other. The graphic designer needs the accountant who needs the hair stylist who needs the landscaper. What all these people have in common is more time than money. They'd rather design, account, style, or landscape in exchange for what they need than pay for it. Your bartering service will allow them to do that by acting as a go-between, keeping the records, and attracting new services. You'll make your money by taking a cut of each transaction, charging membership fees, or a little of both.

Referral Service

Research businesses in a number of fields (child care, plumbing, bed and breakfasts, dentistry, auto repair, etc.) in your area. When you're satisfied that you've found highly skilled, reputable businesses, advertise yourself as a referral service. Instead of letting their crossed fingers do the walking, people can call you for referrals to recommended businesses.

Either the business or the client pays you a small fee or a percentage of the cost of the services that are performed.

Consulting

This is a huge field. There are consultants working in fields as diverse as business creativity, sexual harassment, disability claims, telecommuting, safety, team building, and, of course, every facet of management. If you've got the expertise (and wardrobe) to solve some of your clients' problems or assuage their fears, you can suck the lifeblood of a corporation while claiming to serve it. More power to you. (Information about computer consultants, who barely need expertise or wardrobe, can be found in the computer chapter on page 51.)

Coupon Newsletter Publishing

Coupons can be a great way for businesses to bring in new clients. If the businesses in your town aren't already deluged with advertising opportunities, this is one they might be interested in. If they're already ad-fatigued and aren't buying any more, you'll have to get creative. Use content (an event calendar, free classifieds, columns, personals), a focus on niche (automotive, retail, restaurants), or lists (use a local charity's mailing list and give them a portion of the proceeds) to differentiate your offering.

Inventory Control

Most small businesses are so busy trying to stay afloat that they don't pay enough attention to annoying-but-crucial details like inventory control. With a bar code reader and a laptop, you can offer inventory control services to small businesses that don't have the time or expertise to do it themselves, though they probably know they ought to graduate from their antiquated paper-and-intuition approach. You can offer periodic services or advise businesses about how to purchase and implement inventory control systems.

Payroll Services

Virtually every small business owner dreads having to do payroll. If you truly, madly, deeply understand any of the commercial payroll software packages, are detail-oriented, completely accurate, entirely dependable, and can gain the trust of a bunch of small business own-ers, you can make a tidy living serving the payroll-phobes.

Direct Mail Services

Direct mail can be an extremely effective marketing technique. Or it can be a complete wash. Although it's impossible to accurately fore-cast any mailing campaign's response rate unless it's been thoroughly tested first, there's a lot you can do to increase its chances of success. You can test, test, and test again. Write benefit-rich copy. Make an irre-sistible offer. Local businesses will be happy to pay for your services...if you get results. You won't be able to compete with the direct market-ing behemoths who charge tens of thousands for their services, but you should be able to carve out a small local niche based on affordability, small-business savvy, or a results-based fee.

Mailing List Management

A good mailing list is often the most valuable asset a business owns, but many businesses don't develop and use these lists to their full poten-tial. You can help them do so by providing mailing list maintenance, development, or brokering services. Consider providing complete mail-ing services, combining this business with direct mail services, and deal-ing with the printer and post office.

Meeting Planning

Corporations, associations, conferences, seminars, and all sorts of assorted groups need their meetings planned. All you need to do is work yourself to the bone to make sure that everything runs smoothly, includ-ing the rooms, catering, travel, speakers, entertainment, and locations. It may not be easy, but if organizing people and things is your idea of a good time, you can build a steady clientele. You might want to start by spe-cializing in bringing meetings to one locale (such as your hometown), serv-ing one kind of business (retreats for real estate companies), or running one type of meeting (river rafting as an executive team-building exercise).

Fund-Raising

If you have connections with charities or service organizations, orga-nizational flair, and the know-how to run fund-raising events and campaigns (everything from writing an attention-getting press release to persuading a caterer to donate her time to the cause), you can take a cut of the money you raise. The usual commission is twenty percent. There are some slimy fund-raisers out there, so if you don't have connections, be prepared for rejection. Once you get your foot in the door, though, you can rely on red-hot testimonials to help you get new clients.

Importer/Exporter

This isn't a business opportunity; it's a way of doing business. We include it because it's sexy (for some reason, people like the idea of being in import/export), and because many "get-rich-quick" authors seem to think that with a little research, a fax machine, and a certain quantity of audacity, you can make good money in import/export. You can start small by bringing a stash of stuff back with you from your travels and then testing it for marketability. There are people who jet around the world buying and selling in small quantities. They don't make big money, but enough to pay for food and loading, airfare to their next destination, and other necessities. It doesn't sound so bad, does it?

Publicity Service

You can sell your skills if you can develop "newsy" occasions for businesses (such as sponsoring an unusual contest, affiliating with a popular cause, releasing an innovative product, or hosting an interesting event), and then get coverage of the occasion in local and trade publications, on radio, and television. Until you build an impressive track record, you might want to charge by the coverage you get, instead of by the hour. There are dozens of books about running publicity campaigns. Read them, offer your affordable services to small businesses, and start slowly.

Purchasing Consultant

Large companies have full-time purchasing people who spend their days checking prices and quality, and, of course, going to meetings. Smaller companies have someone who picks up the closest catalog, checks if they can order through an 800 number, and calls. If pricing office supplies is your idea of fun, you can be an out-sourced purchasing consultant. If you're a tree-hugger, you can focus on ecologically correct supplies from paper to lightbulbs to low-flow toilets that will save your clients money and the earth some wear and tear.

Secretarial Services

If you blushingly admit that you sort of like all that secretarial stuff, except for bosses, office politics, and nylons/neckties, you can start a secretarial service. Your market will be home-based and small startup businesses that don't have the cash to hire a secretary and can't fax, type, enter data, or write a simple business letter. We've both worked as temporary secretaries and have been happily astonished that virtually all our bosses, from lawyers to real estate moguls to empty corporate suits, were functionally illiterate. You can increase your income by offering personalized telephone-answering services as well.

Computers

THE THREE BEST THINGS about starting a computer business are: being young is not a disadvantage, you can make tremendous heaps of money, and you only have to know about 15 percent more than your clients to be an expert. Here are twenty-one business ideas that will get you started on the road to Gatesian fame and fortune.

World Wide Web Page Development

We personally hold the WWW in special disregard. Until we have a T1 line running into our living room, it is just too damn slow to be useful. But despite our unhip, Luddite opinion, there's no question that it's here to stay. And there is no lack of companies and individuals who are paying premium prices to be hooked up...and you can make good money by obliging them.

We have several friends and family members making excellent money developing Web pages. In addition to easy money, it can be easy work if you can absorb HTML and have graphic design skills. But because there is increasing competition in this business, here are some ideas about how to stay ahead:

- Specialize in one business type: anything from religious bookstores to tattoo parlors to custom furniture makers.

- Offer cooperative marketing for clients. If you've developed a Web page for a dozen Buddhist bookstores, offer to take out an ad in Buddhist and New Age magazines and newsletters with the Web page's address if each of them pays a fraction of the cost. Your clients will benefit from the exposure.

- Focus on your local area. If you've developed Web pages for twelve of twenty-seven bars in your town, the other fifteen should be easy to sell. After all, who wants to be left out?

We should also mention that an increasing number of businesses exist only online. Besides the flower shops, bookstores, and computer product suppliers, there are also quilt stores, referral services, technical writing companies, and just about every other kind of business. That's not to say that they're making any money online—but they are out there, and all hope that the reality will eventually catch up with the hype.

Computer Consulting

You can focus on hardware, software, the Internet, or a particular service. Small businesses are a ready market for many computer consulting businesses. They can't afford a full-time geek, and will pay you for troubleshooting, advice, and all-around digital wisdom. You can specialize in:

- **Hardware/Software Buying,** working with businesses and individuals to determine their needs, discovering how to best fill those needs, and being involved to some degree with the actual purchasing (pricing and evaluating systems and distributors).

- **Training,** targeting any niche you choose—wealthy technophobes, people working in real estate/non-profit/church/business who use specialized computer stuff. Teach them how to use unfamiliar technology.

- **New Systems,** working with businesses that are converting to new systems, to ease the inevitably torturous transition.

- **Networking,** as an on-call network manager for companies that can't afford to hire a permanent one.

- **System Integration,** focusing on compatibility problems.

- **Databases,** creating, customizing, or improving company databases.

- **Multimedia,** guiding companies that want to develop or use multimedia products for training, publication, or presentations. You can also offer Multimedia Production and actually make the products.

- **Security,** ensuring that no one can hack into a company's system and do dastardly deeds.

- **The Internet**. You can be a freelance Webmaster and design, update, and manage a company's Web sites, or even develop a stable of businesses whose Web sites you administer in exchange for a percentage of goods sold. Or you can be a Netscanner, endlessly searching cyberspace for useful information or business opportunities for your clients.

The most important step with all of these businesses is the one that first gets you through your client's door. Virtually every business has had a bad experience with an antisocial or ineffective techie. If you can prove you're different, they'll probably be happy to keep hiring you for additional jobs. And it pays to focus more on the "social" than the "effective" part—clients rarely know what's wrong with their computer systems, but always have a clear idea what's wrong with their consultants' personalities.

BBS

There are something like 50,000 public Bulletin Board Services in the U.S. But there's still room for one or two more. If you can find a special-interest group that's not being served by a BBS, you have the first ingredient for a membership-based BBS. Or if you know of a group that supports an active local BBS in another area, you may be able to duplicate its success in your area. Steady membership fees are the key, so you've got to provide great content and services to compete against the big boys.

Information Service

"Information overload" has become a cliché, but the problem isn't the amount of information so much as the lack of organization. You'll need to know how to sift through the mountains of available information—primarily through online databases but also through phone contacts—and present the results in a coherent, useful fashion. Because of the vast amount of information, and the requirements of niche marketing, you'll want to specialize in one area, such as one type of demographic, medical, legal, business, or consumer information, for example.

Backup Service

Companies have a tremendous amount of time and money invested in their computer files. But most of them don't back them up, so a virus, fire, or system crash could be incredibly costly. Your job is to back up their files regularly, either by going to their location and doing it in person, or using communications software to do a remote backup. This business works best as an add-on to another computer business.

Data Conversion

Companies change software platforms with some regularity. They need to transfer all their data from software A into software B. Although many applications allow conversion, most of them don't translate perfectly—unless you baby-sit and tweak the process. This is another business that works primarily as an add-on.

Computer Maintenance

You can offer any level of computer maintenance, from cleaning keyboards and wiping down screens to getting inside the computer and cleaning the innards, to running diagnostic tools and configuring systems toward greater efficiency. You can offer the same type of service for laser printers and other office machines.

Data Recovery/Virus Control

If you know how to recover data from overwritten, erased, crashed, burned, battered, or infected drives, and like to see normally restrained business types close to tears, this could be the business for you. They come to you when all hope is lost. If you're successful, you're a hero. If not, you still get paid.

Software Development/Debugging

Although there's an increasing amount of competition for programming jobs, you can specialize in an obscure language or in clients with uncommon needs, such as users of archaic or orphaned systems. Because many companies hire programmers who do a half-assed job, or the company is only halfway committed to using them and doesn't give them enough time to do the job right, there are plenty of opportunities in debugging as well.

Or, if you've got a great idea for a game, utility, or other program, you might think of attempting the retail market. This seems to work best as a startup when you've either developed an add-on to an existing application with a loyal following or have sufficient cash or techie friends to produce a truly professional product. This is one of the few businesses that can be promoted primarily over the Internet. Look into producing a shareware version of your product as a "free sample," but don't make it so limited as to be useless—you'll make no sales and no friends.

Used Computer Broker/Sales

If you know the resale value of every computer you've ever met (including printers, modems, CD-ROMs, and memory/video cards), you can follow the ultimate precept of business success: buy low and sell high. As more selling is done through the Internet, you can pick up bargains there and resell them in your woefully backward hometown. You can also get clients first and then look for computers that fit their requirements.

Disk Duplicating/CD-mastering/Scanning Service

It's unlikely that you can make a full-time income with any of these, but with proper promotion they can provide good part-time money. With disk duping you can also make labels and retail boxes, shrink-wrap items, and ship them—basically becoming a fulfillment service for small software companies. CD-mastering is really a facet of multimedia production, but it can stand alone, especially if you are just compiling single CD-ROMs. If offering scanning services, you will probably want to work with businesses (such as real estate, publishing, and law offices) that have old text documents they'd like to scan into the computer, but don't want to pay to have them retyped.

Graphic Design

Although you can be a highly paid graphic designer with a minimum of art skills, it's becoming increasingly difficult to do so with a minimum of computer skills. Graphic design is an increasingly competitive and specialized field. But it's also still growing, and with a little marketing savvy you won't have too difficult a time finding clients.

In addition to designing Web Pages, you can design business forms, ads, brochures, posters, reports, proposals, greeting cards, newsletters, resumes, logos, books and CD covers, invitations, presentation graphics, signs, menus, programs, tests, and direct mail packages. It's best to focus on a limited number of types of design or industries, such as making forms for college admissions departments or doing brochures for non-profits.

Computer-Aided Design Service

You can design computer models of buildings, clothing, rooms, products, streets, landscaping, plumbing, or just about anything else that's three-dimensional. You can work with professionals involved with any of these industries to help them develop and present their ideas.

Crafts

CARVING A SMALL BUT PROFITABLE NICHE for yourself in the world of crafts requires ingenuity and persistence, but it's an attainable and rewarding goal. If you work with your hands as well as your head, here are twelve business ideas and over 100 other suggestions for ways to make a living by making a craft.

Arts and Crafts Products

Profitable craft products can range from appliquéd T-shirts to leather gear for the sexually adventurous to exotic wood kaleidoscopes. Although it's impossible to list all the objets d'craft out there, here's a list of possibilities to get you started:

Anklets	Birdbaths	Candles
Aprons	Birdhouses	Candlesticks
Babushkas	Blouses	Carvings
Baby blankets	Bookends	Chairs (painted, rocking, high)
Baby carriers	Bookshelves	
Backpacks	Boxes (jewelry, toy, special)	Children's clothing
Baskets		Children's toys
Bat-houses	Bracelets	Children's playhouses
Bathmats	Bridal gowns	Clocks
Belts	Building blocks	Coasters
Bird cages	Bumper stickers	Coats
Bird feeders	Buttons	Cradles

Curtain ties
Curtains
Cutting boards
Dishes
Dolls
Doll clothes
Doll furniture
Doll houses
Dresses
Drug paraphernalia
Duffel bags
Earrings
Egg cups
Eyebrow rings
Fire screens
Folk art
Furniture (children's, garden, home office, bedroom, etc.)
Gardening tools
Hair ornaments
Handbags
Hats
Holiday items
House numbers
Kimonos
Kites
Lamps
Lampshades
Lawn ornaments
Leatherwork
Masks
Massage tools
Meditation mats
Mirrors

Moccasins
Mug racks
Musical instruments
Napkin holders
Napkins
Necklaces
Ornaments
Pet clothes
Pet toys
Pillows
Piñatas
Placemats
Plant holders
Plaques
Potholders
Potpourri
Pottery
Puppets
Purses
Puzzles
Quilts
Religious items
Rings
Rocking horses
Room dividers
Rugs
Sandals
Sashes
Scarves
Screens
Seatcovers
Sex toys
Shawls
Shirts
Shoe trees

Shoes
Signs
Soapdishes
Socks
Stained glass
Stuffed toys
Suits
Sweaters
Swings
T-shirts
Throws
Ties
Towels
Trays
Vests
Wall hangings
Wallets
Wind chimes
Window boxes
Wooden toys
Wrapping paper
Wreaths
Wrought iron stuff
Yarmulkes

And that's the short list.

When you're dreaming up a product, think in terms of a product line. If you're a ceramicist and have been getting glowing reviews of your toothbrush holders, consider branching out into soapdishes, makeup organizers, bathroom mirrors, dental floss delivery devices, toilet paper whoodingies, contact lens containers, etc.

If you're a crafty sort of person, but don't have a particular craft or product in mind even after you've looked at the above, browse through arts and crafts magazines, wander through craft galleries and shows, and scout out retail stores (decorating, jewelry, clothing, gourmet, whatever takes your fancy). You're not looking for a product to copy, but for a new twist on an established product—a new material, function, size, color, combination, or level of quality. If, in your wandering, you happen upon a chatty store owner with time on her hands, ask for some advice about what sells best, what customers would like but have a hard time finding, etc.

CRAFTS SHOWS

These events are without question the most obvious first stop for budding craftspeople. Displaying at a craft show is relatively cheap, doesn't require a large inventory, and, most attractive, you can learn while you earn. You can get feedback about different products, experiment with new ideas, and immediately measure how price changes affect sales. In other words, you're basically getting paid for doing market research.

We should mention, though, that the feedback you should most enthusiastically respond to is green and has pictures of dead presidents on it. It's easy to talk, but unless people are willing to open their wallets—or definitely *would* open their wallets if only your product were chartreuse instead of cerulean—don't take criticism as the Revealed Word of the Marketplace.

On the other hand, if everyone says, "Your flower pots would be great spittoons, if only they had wider openings," maybe you should rethink your plans, face the facts, and go into the saliva business. Remember, though, that some items will sell in stores and galleries but not at shows, and vice versa.

Variations on Arts and Crafts Shows:

Animal shows	Antique shows	Charity shows
College shows	Community festivals	Ethnic festivals
Gay pride festivals	Home parties	Mall shows
Religious shows	Rodeos	Sports events
State or regional fairs	Swap meets	Women's celebrations

Don't join just because you can, though. You've got to wonder if your "Liquor in the Front, Poker in the Rear" T-shirts will be well received at a Celebrate the Goddess festival. If what you're selling fits in well with the show's theme, though, you might want to try your luck. But some craftspeople advise against ever attending new, unproven shows. They say you ought to wait until the show has a track record before joining. Unless the show is super-affordable or ultraconvenient, and you're just dying to go, that's good advice to follow. Don't get discouraged if your first show or shows don't work out. Keep modifying your product and try to get good advice as to which shows are the best.

Pushcarts

Look into selling your work from a mall cart (or a pushcart in another high-traffic retail location). These carts don't come cheap, and you might have to pay someone to staff the cart if you don't do a craft small enough to produce while at the cart itself. But if you can afford the rent and payroll, have a line of affordable, high-markup crafts, and can rent the cart for the months of November and December to exploit the holiday shopping season, you might want to give it a try. Perhaps you can work cooperatively with other crafters to defray the costs and offer a range of products.

Mail Order

This is another opportunity that can require an excessive amount of startup cash, but people do make it work. (Joel worked for several years with a chairmaker who specialized in eighteenth-century reproductions and advertised exclusively through *The New Yorker* magazine. Each ad cost about $800, and brought in substantially more.)

Gift Stores and Craft Galleries

Unlike the case of fine art galleries, it's not taboo to walk in to craft stores and galleries, introduce yourself to the manager or owner, and tell him or her what you make. If they ask to see it, run out to your car and bring the stuff in—displayed attractively, of course. Know what your wholesale prices are, and make sure you don't lose money every time you sell a piece at wholesale. People do this. After the cost of material and overhead, they end up giving away their labor at below-subsistence wage because they want to get the wholesale accounts. But not you—no, you know that selling a hundred items a month and losing a nickel per item isn't quite as good as selling eight items and making thirty dollars per sale.

A peculiarity of the crafts world is that many stores and galleries will ask you to leave your products with them on consignment. Most established craftspeople won't do this. They'll say "If it's good enough to go in your shop, it's good enough for money up front." They claim that shop owners try harder to sell work they've paid for and say they're not in the business of lending money in the form of inventory to galleries. It's undoubtedly true.

But then, established craftspeople are, well, *established*—they don't have to roll over and bark to get their work into a store. We think that with a proper consignment agreement and a judicious follow-through procedure (nagging them often, but not often enough to make them mad), consignment can work for you. It's not a preference; you should definitely ask the store to pay up front. But it's better than having your entire inventory of ox-wool socks molder in your basement.

An alternative to consignment that you can suggest is "selling on approval." You leave a certain number of pieces in a store for a certain length of time (usually sixty or ninety days), at the end of which the store pays you for whatever sold plus any additional pieces they want to keep. You take the rest back. Your inventory isn't tied up indefinitely, the buyer has incentive to move your work without having to take a financial risk, and once your work proves its value, you'll be paid up front.

Designers, Trade Shows, Catalogs, and Reps

If you have appropriate crafts, you may be able to sell through interior designers. It helps tremendously if you can claim a mutual friend—

so ask your friends' parents and your parents' friends if they've worked with an interior designer. Once you've wheedled some appointments, ask the designers if they're interested in your product. If it's not right for them, ask how it could be improved, or what kinds of things they would like to see. And once you're working with one happy interior designer, you can ask her or him to introduce you to another, and another, and...

Trade shows can move you into the big leagues once you've established reasonable, profitable, and tested wholesale pricing, and—this is important—the ability to fill a larger order than you've ever had before, by a not-too-distant deadline. This is not a step to take until you've perfected your product and fulfillment system. Once you have, though, ask people who make similar products which trade shows work best for them, research shows in craft magazines, and take the leap.

The same goes for catalogs, which are basically wholesale mail order. They're a huge market—more than 12 billion catalogs are mailed annually in the U.S. alone. Find catalogs that carry crafts similar to yours, or non-craft items targeted at the same buyers (custom car seat covers in an upscale auto accessories catalog, for example). They'll want discounts of 50 to 70 percent, but that's not so bad considering that they provide the mailing lists, graphics and design, copywriting, and order fulfillment.

Another wholesale strategy is using reps. Although having a number of good reps can free up your time for making your craft, they charge a commission of 15 to 25 percent of the wholesale price. If you're sales-phobic, reps might be the way to go. Be sure that you can make a profit selling your work for about 35 to 40 percent of the retail price and do some serious interviewing and reference-checking before you decide to work with a rep. Try to work out a six-month agreement so you can evaluate the results without tying up your product for too long.

Tradecraft: Service-Based Crafts

The line between product-based craft businesses and service-based craft businesses is a thin one. If you make baby booties by the dozen to sell in craft galleries and baby clothing stores, you're in the product business. But if you're the Baby Tailor, taking orders for custom-made baby outfits, or if you specialize in repairing baby clothes, you're in the service business. Basically, if you're selling your expertise—your ability to make something—more than the thing itself, you're in a service business.

Customization

Most craft products are eminently customizable, especially products like wedding gowns and rings, furniture that has to fit into a certain room, children's playhouses, and musical instruments. You can also custom-make products that aren't always appropriate for sale in craft shows and galleries, such as kayaks, bicycles, doghouses, skis, treehouses, stone fences, painted cars, and so on.

Repair

- Appliances: you get poorly working appliances for free by offering to take them off their owners' hands and then repair them for resale.

- Furniture: stripping, caning, upholstering, refinishing, and repair. Buy unfinished, antique, used, or ugly furniture and finish, fix, and prettify.

- Vehicles: from bicycles to rollerblades to motorcycles to cars, they're always falling apart and in need of repair or maintenance.

- And more: jewelry, musical instruments, tools, dolls, watches, books, clothing, cameras, etc.

Craft-Related Businesses

If you like crafting but aren't interested in working as a craftsperson, you might want to start a craft-related business. Your options look a whole lot like the art-related businesses: teaching, organizing classes, repping, starting a mini-gallery, or managing a cooperative gallery.

If those businesses don't appeal, you can try your hand at selling kits. This is a craft-related business that keeps many crafty entrepreneurs afloat. Although some categories of craft are saturated—such as selling woodworking project kits—there are always smaller niches or new crafts to service. Your kits (again, think in terms of a product line) can require any level of work by the purchaser, from simple assembly to complex construction.

Data and Figures

IF YOU ENJOY WORKING WITH NUMBERS, you can become part of a small but well-paid minority. All you need is a steady supply of math-phobic clients, and one of the following five business possibilities, and you'll be counting all the way to the bank.

Bookkeeping

This is the ultimate data and figures business. If you like record-keeping, reconciling bank statements, and dealing with accounts payable and receivable, to mention just a few of the duties of a book-keeper, then you're a sick puppy. But an important puppy—small business owners will pay a healthy hourly rate to have all those headaches removed. Networking is a great way to get business, and attention to detail (and the tax code), honesty, and reliability will bring you repeat customers. You'll need to look into the licenses or certifications that are required for some kinds of bookkeeping activities.

College Financial Aid Consultant

The amount of financial aid college students receive seems arbitrary. That's because the formula the colleges use to determine the students' financial need is, well, goofy. If students and their families don't know what that formula is, it's a pretty safe bet that they'll get less than they ought to. If they work with a financial aid consultant, however, they can reposition their incomes and assets and get the maximum amount of aid to which they are entitled—and they'll be happy to pay you from their savings. There are books that explain how to maximize financial aid awards, government forms and formulas that are yours for the asking, and prepackaged business opportunities that tell you what you need to know for this business.

Credit Counseling

We like this business because it sounds like setting the fox to guard the hens. What you do is find someone who is desperately in debt (throw a stick, you'll hit a client), and negotiate with his or her creditors to develop a workable payment schedule. If you've scraped the bottom of the barrel for clients, the creditors will have to assume that some payment is better than the only alternative...bankruptcy. Both your client and the creditors pay you about 10 to 15 percent of the debt for your services. (By the way, don't take plastic.)

Math/Tax/Bookkeeping Tutor

People actually want to learn these things. If you actually want to teach them, just find those people. This is difficult to establish as a full-time business, but can be profitable as an add-on business.

Tax Preparation

Maybe you can specialize in legal forms like sole proprietorships or S Corporations, or gear your service to groups like bowlers or recently divorced people. Yes, we know that the tax code is the same for everybody except rich folks and multinational corporations, but people would still rather use a service that panders exclusively to their group. This is seasonal work, so you'll want to keep body and soul together with some other business, such as bookkeeping, as well.

Domestic Businesses

SOME OF THE MOST REWARDING (not to mention challenging and competitive) businesses are oriented around the home and hearth. As are some of the simplest. Here are sixteen businesses that cover the range.

Baker

If you can make terrific breads, cookies, focaccia, brownies, cakes, muffins, or other baked goods, you can rent a commercial kitchen, perfect your recipe, and sell your food retail or wholesale. (Try renting cheap hours before a restaurant opens—you may last a little while without a commercial kitchen, but the health department probably doesn't have much of a sense of humor about that sort of thing.) Selling baked goods is not unlike selling a craft—you can even set up booths at shows. But you probably want to wholesale to delis, restaurants, gourmet food stores, produce markets, and other food retailers. With consistently high quality, reliable delivery, and the proper wholesale prices, you can get baked for a living. You can also specialize in cake decoration, making theme cakes for children's birthdays, graduations, retirement parties, showers, weddings, or holidays.

Breakfast-in-Bed Service

Contract with a restaurant in town, or make your own gourmet breakfasts, and serve them to clients celebrating a special occasion, usually an anniversary or birthday. It's a whole lot more memorable than flowers.

Caterer

This is a tough business. But if you love cooking, organizing, and shmoozing, you can make it work. Start small and focused. Because your product is food, you can specialize in a style—Greek, vegetarian, Japanese, seafood—as well as a client or event type. One way to start very small is to offer brown bag lunch services to businesses in your area, making sandwiches and other lunch foods and then wandering through offices, or taking orders in the morning and delivering them at lunchtime.

Child Care

Families still have a tough time finding child care they're happy with. Although there are licenses to get, regulations to comply with, and you certainly won't get rich, starting a child care service can meet their needs and yours if you like the sound of piping little voices.

Garage/Estate Sale Coordinator

Many people want to have a garage sale without the hassle of actually organizing one. Or they need to have an estate sale but don't want to watch their heirlooms pawed over by the unwashed masses. They hire you, for a percentage of the proceeds or a flat rate, to organize it for them. You do display and promotion, and work with them on pricing.

Housecleaning

If cleaning is your life, you can make a good living indulging your neurosis. Word of mouth is the ultimate marketing tool for housecleaners, so if you scrub like a madperson and go the extra mile, you'll find yourself in demand. In addition to general cleaning, you can advertise your skills at cleaning basements, closets, windows, gutters, bathrooms, recently vacated rental units, and other mess-prone spots.

Other Cleaning

There are all kinds of cleaning opportunities outside of the home. Cars, boats, motorcycles, and planes need cleaning, maintenance, and detailing. So do pools and jacuzzis. Businesses have acoustical ceilings, air ducts, and carpets that need cleaning. You can also offer a toy cleaning service, where you contract with daycare centers, kindergartens, doctors' offices, and other places to periodically clean/sterilize playthings.

Cloth Diaper Cleaning

We've probably all read the statistics about disposable diapers—they're overflowing the landfills and threaten to bury us all. So concerned parents are switching to cloth diapers. But then they have to clean the little toxic bundles. *Yurg!* If the olfactory centers in your brain are not too sensitive, you can help eco-friendly but squeamish parents by offering a cloth diaper cleaning service. You have a route, pick up the dirty goods, and return them sparkling clean.

Errand Service

This is another service for the temporally challenged. If your clients haven't got the time to buy groceries or gifts, pay the bills, or fill the car with gas, you do it for them and charge by the hour. Or you can specialize as a children's taxi. When parents work and aren't able to cart their kids around, they hire you. This business is easily combined with entertaining children, child care, or other children-oriented businesses.

Event Planner

This business also takes advantage of people's busy schedules. You can organize children's, retirement, anniversary, engagement, divorce, graduation, or other parties. You can do baptisms, confirmations, bar/bat mitzvahs, weddings, or showers. If you want to thrive on other people's misery, consider becoming a class reunion planner.

Florist/Flower Arranger

You can't compete with national delivery services and their low, low prices. But by offering personalized service to a unique niche, you can make flower-selling and arranging work.

Gift Buying Service

For some reason, we hate this idea. But you have to admire people who make their living by shopping with other people's money. So...market to people (like lawyers) who have plenty of money but no time to shop for the perfect gift. Get a list of occasions for which they'll need presents—anniversaries, birthdays, holidays—and the recipients' preferences. Then buy and deliver the gifts, and charge the clients.

Menu Service

People know how important good nutrition is, but they don't know how to plan healthy, tasty menus. If you do, create weekly or monthly menus based on your clients' specific needs. You can target a group of people with the same specific needs. In addition to working for individuals, you can target schools, restaurants, hospitals, nursing homes, and the like—there are certification issues here, so do your research!

Home Design Consultant

With a flair for design, you can use anything from decorative wall finishes to antique furniture to skylights to take clients' homes one step closer to their ideal. Although you have to make sure you're not violating licensing laws, you can offer many of the same services as an interior decorator. Because you'll have less overhead and no expertise other than your impeccable taste and knowledge about where to buy what, you will probably have to be relatively cheap unless you're credentialed or specializing in an area that justifies high prices. Or you can just focus on better displaying the stuff clients already have—moving the couch here and that picture over there, maybe throwing away those curtains...

Personal Chef

Without spending too much more than they would at an expensive restaurant, your clients can have you come to their homes and cook them a gourmet meal. It can be more romantic than dinner out and much more memorable. If you can build a regular clientele of wealthy people who want a home-cooked gourmet meal every week or month, this can become a solid business. Otherwise, you'll want to combine this with another food or home-oriented business.

Senior Services

If you like old people, you're in luck: there are many of them around, and they have need of home care, daily visits, meal delivery/cooking, shopping, and transportation, to name just a few services you can offer. But, of course, if there's a demand, you can also offer sax lessons, travel services, or bungee jumping. This isn't really its own business as much as a very large and possibly lucrative niche for other businesses to serve.

Wedding Consultant

A wedding is basically just a huge outlay of cash wrapped in a poofy dress, frosted and surrounded by flowers and matching napkins. But someone's got to organize it. If you can organize the caterer, florist, musicians, mothers-in-law, and weather while making sure that the right people get corsages and the wrong people don't, you can make a bundle.

Eco-Businesses

DEVELOPING A SMALL BUSINESS that heals the earth combines the best of two worlds: the world of green, and the world of green. Although there are only six specific businesses listed, most other businesses can be made environmentally sound by following the principles we mention below.

RECYCLING

A recycling business can be one of the old standbys: paper, glass, or aluminum recycling. Or it can be a little less traditional, such as turning discarded tires into fuel, asphalt, building materials, and sandals; mining old computers for the raw materials of clocks, binders, and key chains; or processing old telephone directories into insulation and kitty litter.

Unfortunately, some recycling opportunities require technology, cash, and know-how. If you want to turn industrial waste into drywall or styrofoam peanuts into orthopedic in-soles, you've got to have all sorts of obscure knowledge. Here are some recycling careers that don't require unusual skills.

Using Recycled Materials

You can incorporate recycled materials into many art or craft businesses. Make belts out of old bottle tops, jewelry out of used glass, or birdhouses from used computer parts. You can even carve out a small niche for yourself in the competitive world of paper recycling by making artsy handmade paper. There are many people who have combined crafting and recycling to create unique, lucrative, and green businesses.

Recycling Consultant

You can set up recycling programs for companies. Many of them would like to be (or seem) more eco-friendly, and if they can do it with a minimum of hassle, they will. You can sell or rent recycling bins, arrange for pickup by a recycling company, and even make weekly rounds to organize the recyclables.

Recycled Art Supplies

We know of an art supply store that sells only recycled materials, such as used milk crates, chair wheels, odd-sized particle board, industrial adhesives, and overstocked doll parts. You can develop a network of businesses that will give you any interesting trash they generate. You also need to know what artists like, and have an overpopulation of artists in your area. One benefit of selling recycled supplies to artists is that you don't need to have an upscale storefront—an empty garage will do until the neighbors complain.

Green Products Retailer

There are an increasing number of stores that sell only green products. Although retail can be prohibitively costly, you might be able to sell through mall carts, by renting space in an existing store, or by selling at fairs and festivals. You'll need products that are attractive impulse buys and can bear a good markup.

RENEWING

A renewing-oriented business is much like a recycling one. The difference is that a renewed product becomes the same-only-better; a recycled product becomes something totally different.

The most obvious way to renew something is simply to fix it up. People often throw out furniture, appliances, clothes, and other objects you can recondition. Refurbish it, decorate it, and you've transformed landfill fodder into a better-than-new product. A good place to find freebies is in the classified ads. Many people will give you all sorts of borderline-quality stuff for free if you offer to haul it away. Another great source of reusables is the dump.

Any service that extends the life of a product works against the kind of throw-away consumerism that makes Captain Planet wring his hands.

Almost any sort of repair is better than relegating salvageable material to the junkheap.

REDUCING

A reducing business focuses on reducing consumption and waste or on reducing the use of or exposure to toxins.

Eco-Purchasing/Energy Efficiency Consultant

The number of ecologically correct products is becoming bewildering. You can help concerned citizens locate the most appropriate office and home supplies and show them that it *is* easy being green. You can also introduce businesses to energy-efficient lightbulbs, low-flow water devices, pre-owned office furnishings, and the like. In addition to (or in place of) an up-front fee, you can agree to take a portion of the savings you generate, usually the difference between the average utility bill before and after your services, for a certain period of time. You can also show people how to reduce water and electricity use in their households and get paid for your time as well as any eco-friendly products you sell.

Another way to think about energy efficiency is to focus on behaviors instead of products. Is there a way you can change people's behavior, be environmentally sound, and make a buck in the process? Some examples of this are van-pool or telecommuting consulting services.

Other Reducing Ideas

There are an increasing number of opportunities if you're interested in reducing the messes we've been making. You can offer radon-testing services, deal with "sick-building syndrome" through anything from consulting to environmentally correct carpet cleaning, or sell any of the large variety of air and water filtration systems.

Or you can reduce the use of toxic chemicals and environmentally unsound practices in the first place by breeding and selling natural predators instead of pesticides, starting a cloth diaper cleaning business, or making and/or selling any sort of green alternative to a mainstream pollutant.

Although there aren't many traditional small businesses in this area, there's plenty of room for growth and innovation. So innovate. And when you've come up with novel, effective small business ideas, drop us a line. We'd love to hear about them.

Health

ENTREPRENEUR, **HEAL THYSELF**. There are innumerable opportunities to make money as a healer. Most of them we pass over briefly in the section on being an alternative health practitioner. But there are eight other small business possibilities for caring entrepreneurs to choose from, as well.

Alternative Health Practitioner

The options are endless. We're lumping together holistic health careers in a brief section, because we don't have the space to include a complete list, and just want to give you an idea of what's possible.

Some states require licenses in order to practice certain alternative health techniques. The closer you are to the goofy fringe of alternative health, the less likely you'll have to comply with governmental red tape—we can't imagine the state-certified test for aura cleansers, for example. There are, though, certification courses, some as rigorous as traditional medical certification courses, for most alternative health practitioners. We recommend you take them if this interests you, since if you're messing about with a client's body and psyche, you ought to know what you're doing. Alternative health techniques and methods include massage, yoga, colonic irrigation (if you don't know, don't ask), shamanism, breathwork, any of the many schools of bodywork, aromatherapy, herbalism, and much, much more.

One of the advantages of starting a healing business is that most healers believe that the three most important marketing techniques are good posture, affirmations, and being a nice person. And that's all the marketing that they do. That's like saying that the three most important health techniques are smiling, developing a steady income, and flossing. They're important, but if you're drinking Mountain Dew and eating pork rinds for every meal, you're missing the point. If you're a healer, also be a marketer—imagine how many more people you'll have an opportunity to help.

Astrology/Tarot/Divination

It was good enough for Nancy and Ron Reagan—it'll be good enough for your clients, too. Read the stars, cards, palms, tea leaves, auras, spirits, or anything else more intelligible to you than to others. If you're mediocre, your business will fizzle out. If you're terrific and professional, you can charge very impressive fees and people will wait in line to pay them.

New Parent Services

First-time parents are often uneasy, even terrified, about the approaching blessed event. If you've been through it all already, or have nursing or midwife experience, your classes and personal counseling as a childbirth instructor can help make childbirth as positive an experience as possible. If you're not fully credentialed and aren't working through OB/GYN offices or hospitals, you might want to focus on something they don't provide, such as seminars about the merits of non-traditional approaches to childbirth, home visits, or pre- and postpartum exercise and nutrition classes.

Working as a Lactation Consultant is a natural add-on business for a childbirth instructor, although some states require certification or a nursing or related degree. Apparently breast-feeding isn't as easy as it looks, and many new mothers are doing it painfully and incorrectly. Teach them the proper technique with patience and knowledge, and you should benefit from word of...mouth referrals.

There are many other, more mundane new parent services you can offer: anything that helps your clients adjust to their new sleep-, time-, and social life-deprived lifestyle may be in demand.

Childproofing Service

When the little ones get mobile, it's time to remove everything from the house except the pillows and beanbag chairs. Parents will pay you to crawl around like a baby, making sure that nothing dangerous remains. It's not just sharp objects, though—you'll also want to check houseplants (the leading cause of poisoning in the home), toxic bathroom and kitchen cleaning chemicals, that clear varnish in the apple juice bottle, etc. Selling childproof products is a natural add-on.

Exercise Coach/Personal Trainer

You can work through a health club or two, offering your services to their members, work out of your home, or go mobile and conduct classes at clients' homes. Think about targeting a niche market or two: women who have recently had babies, golfers, or people with a particular health condition (HIV, high blood pressure, arthritis, etc.).

Health Product Sales

There are any number of health products out there, many of which actually work. You can sell anything from blue-green algae to massage tools to fresh-squeezed wheatgrass juice. Competition is fierce, so unless you have an exclusive area for a truly wonderful new product, this idea works best as an add-on to another business.

Sports Coach

If you not only excel at a sport, but understand why you excel at it, you can make money teaching it. You can offer classes or one-on-one instruction—you'll probably need to offer both. Find a market and then custom-design a class for it: offer karate for seniors, paragliding for compulsive hand-washers, or basketball for spiritual seekers. Of course, there are also less active sports that people will pay to learn, including billiards, target shooting, bowling, and darts.

Weight Loss Coach

Weight loss is a huge business, not surprising since most Americans look Jabba-like in their underwear. Work with a client to develop a reasonable weight loss regimen based on the oh-so-boring-but-effective principles of exercise, eating well, and reasonable expectations. Then enforce it with dictatorial strictness when they're having trouble hauling their lazy asses off the couch, and you'll have a thriving business. It's as easy as taking candy from an adult.

Language and Writing

YOU DON'T HAVE TO BE A LITERARY GENIUS to make a living with writing (actually, it helps if you're *not* a genius). You just have to pay attention to detail, have a solid understanding of editing, or be able to write understandable prose. If you can do any of the above, here are sixteen business ideas for you.

Abstracting Service

In addition to performing freelance work for publishers, you can solicit corporations that have a vested interest in a field and offer to provide them with abstracts of all the relevant articles in the appropriate trade journals. You'll probably want to specialize in a field in which you have a strong background. This works best as an add-on to another writing business, because it often pays poorly. But then, the work's not so hard to begin with, and can help you fill in the cracks between other projects.

Book Indexer

If you're sufficiently detail-oriented, love books, and have a masochistic urge to be part of the glamorous world of publishing, this could be for you. You work with a nonfiction book in the final stages of pre-publication and, well, index it. If you do a consistently great job, you'll get repeat business and referrals.

Editor/Proofreader

In addition to working with publishers, which tend to have a surplus of prospective editors, you can work with a better-paying clientele: semi-literate businesspeople. Businesses produce everything from brochures to annual reports to press releases, and if they don't have someone on staff who specializes in such things, you can train them to fax or e-mail their writing to you for editing before it's sent to the printer. There's also a new world of online editing opening up, as more businesses create Web pages. It's recently become possible to make a living by helping Webmasters polish the prose on their sites.

Essay Coaching/College Application Coach

No, you won't write the whole thing for them, at least not at your regular rate. But many prospective college students can use all the coaching they can get to produce a college application essay that is recognizable as English. This is a seasonal business, so you'll want to have something else going as well. And if you can get hooked up with the hearts and wallets of prospective students from other countries, you can start a mini-empire.

Interpreter/Translator/Foreign Language Instruction

If you know a foreign language or sign language fluently, are able to provide near-simultaneous interpretation, and live in a largish city, you can provide interpretation services for tourists, businesspeople, and speakers. If you have writing skills as well, you can offer translation services, primarily translating business communications. Think of specializing in a business area, such as computer manufacturing and sales. You can also offer classes teaching your language skills.

Resumé Service

Although resumés may not be the best way to get jobs (and although jobs aren't the best thing to get), they are one of the most common. Set yourself apart by offering specialized paper, quick turnaround, and the ability to post resumés on line. These are all in addition to your brilliant organizational and writing skills, of course.

WRITER

Fiction writing is the biggie. And it's not just any fiction—the vast majority of wannabe writers hope to write the next *English Patient*. Well, even in the unlikely case that you can write deathless prose, you still oughtn't think of it as a viable business. You're as likely to make money writing "literary" fiction as you are creating fine art. It could happen. But as far as a business goes it makes a great hobby.

Writing genre fiction—mystery, romance, science fiction, adventure—is another story. That's because there's a ready market for it. Unfortunately, in a world of supply and demand, writing any kind of fiction is the worst sort of gamble. If you can turn out a genre novel that's the-same-only-different, you have a small chance of making it. If you can turn one out every two months, you have a better chance.

If fiction writing is your passion, do it. But if you want to treat it in a businesslike fashion, increasing your chances from one in a million to one in a thousand, combine your passion with a little market savvy. Purists will tell you to live with integrity, producing only works of art. Then when you're discovered you'll be hailed as a genius. This does happen (and if it happens to you, you're apparently obliged to drink yourself to death). But we think it's a far better thing to write as well as you can in the genre that most interests you and has a sizable readership.

Nonfiction is a much better bet because there's so much more of it and far fewer people think it's their personal road to fame and fortune. If you want to write nonfiction books, all you need are competent writing skills and a new take (read: niche) on a subject—such as a how-to business book for twentysomething corporate rejects. Still, this isn't usually a road to riches, so you'll want to combine it with other businesses, as you would writing genre fiction. If you like the idea of making a living wage writing nonfiction books, you can offer ghostwriting services. This is tough to do before you have a track record, but it can be done. Or you can combine your nonfiction career with other information businesses—offering seminars and speeches, selling audio- and videotapes, starting a newsletter, and so on.

Many nonfiction writers make a great living by focusing on grants and proposals, technical writing, articles, and copywriting. Others become writers/publishers and produce directories, newsletters, booklets, and even books.

Grant/Proposal Writer

Writing a good grant, and targeting it well, is a very valuable skill. Many nonprofit organizations and individuals who are potential recipients of grant money either don't know it, haven't the time to explore the possibilities, or can't write a quality proposal. If you do, have, and can, you can charge either by the hour, the project, or take a percentage of the grant you raise. You can also write proposals for companies that want to do business with the government, which usually requires a proposal.

Technical Writer

You'll need the technical knowledge to take complex information and translate it into clear instructions for people without specialized backgrounds. Usually the instructions are in the form of a manual, documentation, or presentation, but there's a rapidly growing field of writing online help and documentation as well.

Article Writer

Although it's rare for a writer to make enough money writing articles to pay all the bills, article writing can provide a healthy second income. You'll need to know how to determine what a publication wants before you set pen to paper or finger to keyboard, how to get the most from a topic, and how to resell your writing. Check your library or bookstore to discover the helpful books that describe this process.

Copywriter and Business Writer

There's a law in writing that says the more creative and literary your writing, the less money you make. That's good news for writers who work with businesses. There's a perverse school of copywriting that emphasizes creativity, which is why you see so many interesting ads that don't make you want to buy anything, but the best copywriting is aimed straight at the reader's wallet. If you can write clear copy that makes people want to buy a product right now, you can make very good money for yourself. Focus on ad, direct mail, or even radio copy. If writing sales copy isn't your thing, you can focus on business plans, annual reports, or other corporate communications.

PUBLISHER/SELF-PUBLISHER

Although you're not going to compete with those multinational leviathan corporate publishers such as Ten Speed Press, you can carve out a lucrative niche for yourself.

Directory publishing can cost a bit to start up due to all the direct mailing it involves. You pick a group of related businesses/organizations, find support/supply businesses in the same field, write to them asking for information, and put it all together in a directory. For example, let's say you want to make a directory of tattoo artists. You want all the tattoo artists you can find, plus people who supply equipment, ink, and designs, tattoo consultants, tattoo magazines, and so on. Combine and stir. If you ensure that it's useful, you can update your directory periodically and sell it all over again. The prices you can charge can be hefty—check out the cost of the smaller directories in your public library. Some publishers charge people for listings in their directory. This smacks of vanity publishing to us, but it makes nice economic sense. It's true that you're counting on vanity to sell most of your books, because your best prospects are the people you've listed.

There are many ways to publish a newsletter. You can create a customized monthly or bimonthly in-house newsletter for a business, covering new hires, awards, policy changes, and events. Or you can start a subscription newsletter, covering information of use and interest to a particular group, such as travel writers, people who bet on horse races, or computer consultants. Almost any niche market you serve is a possible newsletter market, as well.

Publishing booklets is the recommended strategy for getting rich in mail order. We know this because we bought a booklet through the mail that told us. It can work if you write a booklet that focuses on some fundamental human interest—money, sex, beauty, health, love, power, success—and is aimed at a defined group: how you, an antique pen collector, can make more money/have more sex/be more successful. Books aren't all that different than booklets. They're just longer. And if you've got the money to start up a self-publishing business, you probably won't have it for long unless you appeal to one of those same fundamental human interests. There are many books about self-publishing a book. Here's a helpful hint: the writing is the easiest part.

Another possibility for books and booklets is publishing something of regional interest, like a bargain, hiking, or restaurant guide to your area. Then sell it locally, and use it to promote your other, related services.

Music and Performing

NOT ONLY ARE THERE MANY OPPORTUNITIES for musicians and performers, but there are opportunities for people who love music and performing, as well. The following thirty-two business opportunities and performance possibilities can suit anyone interested in playing for pay.

Band Manager

Are you aggressive, organized, and able to find a performer or band with heaps of talent? If so, you can get about twenty percent of everything they bring in by taking care of, well, everything. Get gigs, contact the press, record demos, wipe noses, and generally hustle. Even if you're able to get very regular gigs, it can be extremely hard to live off 20 percent of not much, so you'll want to combine your management with another business until your clients land that big recording contract.

Booking Agent

If you don't want the hassle of working too closely with any one band as a manager, you can work with a whole mess o' bands as a booking agent instead. In exchange for a commission (usually ten percent, sometimes fifteen percent), you set up gigs with as many bands as you can. The same principle works if you're booking non-musical entertainers.

Music/Performing Instructor

From teaching piano to drama to juggling to dance, instruction has always been bread-and-butter income for performers. If you know Afro-Cuban drumming, square dance calling, or flamenco dancing, share the wealth. It's rarely all that lucrative by itself. Think about developing a mail order course complete with videotapes, or offering classes through institutions or at your clients' homes.

Event Entertaining

You can perform at every kind of party and event. If you have skills in clowning, juggling, stage hypnosis, puppetry, stripping, face-painting, singing, impersonation, comedy, dancing, magic, mime, storytelling, or DJ-ing, you can get paid for partying.

Murder Mystery Producer

We never thought this was a workable business idea until we met someone who did it. We still have a hard time believing it, but it apparently works. Arrange with a restaurant or hotel to produce an evening of murder at their location. They provide the dinner and you provide the entertainment: during dinner one of the "guests" is shot, stabbed, poisoned, or done to death in any other novel or gruesome fashion. It's up to your customers (with, perhaps, a little guidance from you) to find out whodunit. All you need is a bunch of actors and costumes, a good plot, a willing location, and a healthy sense of the dramatic.

Equipment and Instrument Repair/Fabrication

This occupation probably belongs in the crafts section, but we put it here on the assumption that many musicians know how to fix their instruments and equipment, and some even know how to make them. If you do, and especially if you've mastered some tricky repairs, spread the word—less enterprising musicians could use your skills.

Seminar/Speech Recording

If you have the equipment, you can hire yourself out recording speeches and seminars. Make contacts through speakers' bureaus, conference facilities, and networking. Unless you live in an area that attracts many conventions, you might have to combine this with other audio services.

Local Compilation Producer

There are probably more bands in your area than there are people interested in local bands. This makes it pretty tough for any band to sell a CD, even locally. But if you develop a compilation featuring several of the best local bands, it will have a much larger market. If you include information in the CD sleeve about all the contributing bands, you can probably talk them into letting you use their songs with no or a very low royalty—they get the benefit of exposure, after all.

Chart Writer

Most musicians can't read or write music. So if they want their genius immortalized on paper, or if they just want to communicate with studio players or other musicians or transpose a part to a different key, they've got to come to you. They come up with the brilliant song ideas, and you write them down.

Demo Packager

Although demos are not necessarily the best way to get discovered, they're one of the most commonly attempted. As a demo packager, you won't be working with the songs themselves, but with the packaging. Help the band produce a professional-quality j-card or CD sleeve, bios, and promotional materials. Tell them how many songs of what length are preferred. And deliver an eye-catching, top-quality demo that will only fail by virtue of the music or the fact that no recording exec ever listens to it.

Equipment Rental/Rental Broker

Bands typically have more money tied up in equipment than they're ever likely to make by performing. If that's you or your friends and colleagues, you can make money by renting out your equipment or working as a clearinghouse of rental information. And because you've got your finger on the pulse of the local music scene, it's not that hard to get the word out. Of course, like many of the music-oriented businesses, that doesn't mean this can provide a full-time living unless you're in an urban area.

Independent Distributor

Every band that lasts long enough records a CD. Then the least-disturbed band member approaches all the local music stores to see if they'll sell it on consignment. This is a hassle for the store managers because 1) They're always being approached by unprofessional freaks with bad teeth, and 2) The record-keeping for a dozen consignment deals is a nightmare. That's where you come in. Arrange with as many bands as you can to distribute their CDs—you'll do a better job than they will, and music stores would much rather deal with one central source.

Independent Label

Start a local label. You're not going to even try to compete with the big boys—just work regionally or with a certain musical style to sell what you can. It's better for bands to be part of even a small effort like yours because it gives them a bit more credibility than releasing their own recording, and you'll handle most of the business annoyances like bookkeeping.

Personalized Song Service

You can write fun, funny, tear-jerking, loving, or vicious songs for people, businesses, organizations, or events. Advertise your services for holidays such as Mother's Day and Valentine's Day and events such as birthdays. Not much of a full-time business, but a nice additional source of income.

MUSICIAN

If you want to make your fortune as a stadium-playing rocker, there are two things you should keep in mind. One, not only do the vast majority of bands never get signed to a label, but the majority of those who do get signed never achieve any level of notoriety or income. Two, most of those who *do* confound the odds by getting signed do so after establishing themselves on a local scene. Sending out demo tapes and crossing your fingers is a one-way ticket to obscurity. If you can develop a rabid regional following, though, you just might be able to parlay that into a recording contract. So for right now, whatever your long-term goals, focus locally.

Playing Events

The most important skills for freelance music success are not musical. Most of the people who will be paying you to play don't know all that much about music. As long as you have the minimum necessary skills, they won't care if you have perfect pitch and more soul than James Brown. They only care about their event going well. Their event goes well if they have music that fits the occasion, and musicians who act like professionals.

The harsh reality is that a musically mediocre band that acts professionally and promotes itself well will get far more business—and far happier clients—than any number of tormented musical geniuses who can't relate.

The first place you probably think of performing is at local bars and clubs. That's fine, but unless you live in a city, don't limit yourself to the obvious. Also consider:

- accompaniment (recitals, choirs, etc.)

- advertising and public relations companies for jingles and events

- associations for dinners, fund-raisers, dances, award ceremonies, and other events

- businesses for grand openings, sales, parties (Christmas, Fourth of July, and New Year's)

- class reunions

- college and student parties (in addition to local campuses, contact the National Association for Campus Activities, Box 6828, Columbia, SC 29260)

- conventions and meetings

- fashion shows given by department stores, boutiques, etc.

- festivals, parades, fairs, parties, and carnivals

- hotels for lounge, lobby, convention, and trade show jobs

- musical telegrams

- restaurants

- shopping malls

- social and civic clubs

- performing on the street or in public spaces, and

- weddings, rehearsal dinners, and receptions

But if you *do* want to focus on playing in bars and clubs, remember one thing: the owner wants to make money. That's it. If you can pull people into the bar and get them to drink (which is where the money is), you'll be invited back. You have to market each of your gigs in a professional manner, not just relying on two dozen posters and haphazard word-of-mouth recommendations. If you can bring in the bodies, you can make money playing clubs.

Plants and Farming

MONEY DOES GROW ON TREES. And stalks, bushes, vines, and stems. If you love plants, one of the following seventeen ideas may be what you're digging for.

GROWING VEGGIES

You don't need vast acreage to be a successful farmer. In fact, most established mini-farms bring in far more profit per acre than huge corporate farming concerns. Small-scale farming can be more than growing veggies for sale at farmers' markets and roadside stands. But it doesn't have to be. Although certainly not a quick road to riches, growing "regular" produce and selling directly to the customer can be a viable and rewarding business. We have a friend who started this very business. Working part-time, he made about $4,000 the first year on a quarter acre. The second year (still part-time), on a half acre, he made between $8,000 and $9,000. This year he expects to make about $14,000 on three-quarters of an acre. And the year after that he'll do even better. Not a fortune, but he's moving in the right direction—due not only to increased acreage, but also improved management because he's using space more efficiently, building soil fertility, timing plantings, and planting more lucrative crops. And it's his passion. Who knows, maybe the bum will be working full-time sooner or later?

Farmers' Markets

Farmers' markets offer many of the same benefits for growers that craft shows do for crafters: minimal startup costs, retail prices, no shipping or packaging hassles, immediate customer feedback, and the opportunity to see what and how your competitors/colleagues are selling. On the other hand, they take a whole lot of time, are dependent on the weather, and can limit the volume of your sales.

Roadside Stands

Roadside stands are another common produce outlet. Location is the key. If you can offer other attractions (such as ten-cent lemonade or a pick-your-own section), you'll multiply your sales.

On-the-Road Stands

Make your stand mobile and sell your veggies off the back of your truck. Target densely populated family neighborhoods with high-demand veggies such as tomatoes and corn. Stay away from congested and commuting areas, though. Give each stop two or three chances before you decide it's not profitable, and then move on. And keep records of how much you sell of each product and when you sell it—maybe you can reduce the hours you work and keep the volume level.

Subscription Farming

With one of the many subscription farming plans, it's possible to sell your produce before you grow it. What all of them have in common is that your customers order and pay for a share of the upcoming season's crop in advance. But beyond that, you can do almost anything:

- charge customers a membership fee ($25 to $50) for the right to pick their own produce on your farm for a premium price.

- harvest the crops and make them available on your farm, deliver them to a central location, or (for a larger fee) to your customers.

- sell shares of your harvest in a Community Supported Agriculture (CSA) plan. Customers pay up front, usually between $250 and $500, depending on the expected size of the harvest, and share in your risk. If the harvest is bad, they don't get their money's worth; if it's great, they get more. Once or twice a week the crops are divided up among the customers. You have to be able to draw on involved people who want to support a local farmer and get fantastic produce.

SPECIALTY CROPS

If your interest is in growing in general, there's more money to be made from specialty crops such as exotic veggies, flowers, and herbs.

Exotic crops range from shiitake mushrooms to jicama to mesclun salad mix to blue potatoes and yellow watermelon. Think about your market before you decide which exotics to grow. Are the people you're targeting health-conscious, ethnic, trendy, upscale, or something else? Farmers' magazines and conferences will tell you what's *expected* to be in demand—and often they're right. But don't put all your eggplants in one basket. Diversify your crops unless you're absolutely sure you've got a winner.

Herbs

Herbs are a big business. Not only can they command a higher price than veggies, but they have many uses in addition to spices: they can be used in tea, soap, jelly, and even herbal wine. You can sell dried herbs, herb pillows, herbal incense, bath oils, potpourri, sachets, and wreaths. This extends your market far beyond that of veggie-growers into craft fairs, home and bath shops, and New Age bookstores.

Flowers

Flowers are another crop that has many possibilities, and it usually pays better than veggies. You can produce cut flowers, flowers in pots, edible flowers, or crafts with dried flowers. Farmers who add just a quarter acre of flowers to cut and sell at farmers' markets can up their gross by several thousand dollars—and pick-your-own flower patches or wholesaling flowers to florists and other retailers increase the gross even more.

Wholesaling

Don't forget that you can wholesale your crops as well. This way of working is most effective with nontraditional crops such as specialty foods or organically grown veggies. Target restaurants, gourmet shops, health food stores, hotels, florist shops, or nurseries. And instead of producing a crop and then busting your butt trying to sell it, you can make phone calls or visits asking what's in demand and then provide it next season.

VALUE-ADDED

Our farmer friend figures he earns about thirty dollars an hour by making salsa out of the veggies that are blemished, too small, or otherwise unsuited for retail sales. That's a whole lot more than he makes doing anything else—typical for value-added products. You can dry, pickle, squeeze, cook, bake, or juice your regular produce to transform it into a high-value, high-demand specialty product. You broaden your product line and use otherwise-unsalable produce at the same time. Some possible value-added products are salsa, sauces, pickles, chutney, jams, juices, baked goods, and dried snacks.

Another way to add value is through packaging and presentation. Ready-to-eat salad mixes and ready-to-stir-fry veggie mixes are two examples of how packaging alone can create new products. You can add value through packaging by changing the quantity of what you're selling—package several varieties of fruit or veggie together in a gift or sample box, sell single stalks of celery instead of by the bunch, or braid stalks of garlic together. Offering recipe cards for less-common produce can make the difference between a passing interest and a sale.

PROCESSING

Many small farms don't do as much processing as they could. That's a pity for them, but could be an opportunity for you. Contact them about buying their seconds—food that's good to eat but not to look at. Then process and package it yourself. You can then sell it as a product at any of the markets mentioned above (plus those mentioned later in the marketing chapters, such as mail order), or as a service. The service is one you offer the farms: after you transform their produce, you sell it back to them at wholesale and they re-sell it retail. They don't have the hassle of adding value themselves, and you don't have the hassle of tending temperamental crops or finding a market.

Local Baby Food

Studies reveal all sorts of pesticide residue in the mass-produced baby foods. If you can make a good, healthy product, comply with food preparation and licensing laws, and get the word out, you can charge a premium and have customers calling you.

Nursery

The startup costs can put this business opportunity out of range unless you have the know-how to do much of the work yourself, but there's plenty of money to be made growing seedlings. In addition to growing regular and specialty veggies, herbs, and flowers, you can try bonsai trees, cacti, or other ornamental plants.

Landscaping

Aside from the old standbys like roto-tilling and regular lawn care, you can offer specialized services such as herb, veggie, rock, balcony, or flower garden design. Once customers see what a good job you do in one area, they will be more than willing to hand over the rest of their garden work to you as well. If you've got a bright green thumb and can figure out what's ailing a sick plant, you can be a plant doctor. Although your patients will usually be trees, you can also do this as a sideline for ailing gardens and indoor plants. And if you can deliver health with organic remedies, so much the better.

Topiary Designer

Topiary, the art of trimming plants to look like big goofy animals, can be a rewarding business. It's unusual enough to be easily promotable through media releases, and can benefit from tremendous word of mouth. Customize your proposals to the company. If you're pitching a lab supply outlet, offer to make their shrubs look like microscopes and flasks. Yeah, it's pretty tacky, but it's also fun and can be lucrative, too.

Office Plant Rental/Care

Offices need plants and plants need tending. You can rent or sell plants to offices and then sell your services to take care of the plants. If you can afford to supply the plants for free, you'll find it fairly easy to get clients, and you can make your money on the upkeep even after you take a loss on the initial investment. Or you can differentiate your business by offering special plants (which are meant to counteract the toxic environment of the office, for example), special services (such as periodically exchanging old plants for new ones), or working with special gatekeepers (such as interior decorators or feng-shui practitioners).

Miscellaneous

IF YOU DON'T WANT TO BE PIGEON-HOLED, this is the pigeon hole for you: miscellaneous. Here are sixteen business possibilities that didn't fit into the other sections, or fit into several of them at once.

Antiques/Collectibles/Vintage Clothing Broker

To start a business as an antique dealer, you need to sink many thousands of dollars into your shop and inventory. As a broker, you work for as many retail dealers and collectors as you can, going to auctions and estate sales, answering classified ads, and looking for a good deal. You've got to know what sort of inventory your clients need as well as how much they'd be willing to pay for any particular item. You buy low and sell slightly less low. Repair and refurbish your purchases to increase your bottom line. Don't think you can only broker Shaker chairs, Hummel figurines, or old mantillas—by specializing in antique tools, glass, tins, and so on, you can develop a national clientele.

Children's Classes

You can teach (or hire other people to teach) crafts, languages, cooking, math, reading, or just about anything else to kids as an after-school activity. Parents are often obsessively interested in ensuring that their children have every possible advantage, so it's your job to tell them that unless little Suzy goes to your classes, she'll be an unemployed crackhead mother of five by the time she hits eighteen. That'll boost your enrollment. Or you can just emphasize the advantages of fun, social, supervised learning.

College Application Consultant

If you can learn the reputations, costs, and strengths and weaknesses of most of the colleges and universities in the country, you can get paid to share your knowledge. Interview prospective students and their parents and help guide them through their college choices. You can also help them fill out those fiendish college application forms, serve as an essay coach, or, if you're good with numbers too, as a financial aid consultant.

Consignment Store

We're leery of any retail store startup idea that requires a hefty stack of cash. But consignment stores have one big benefit: the cost of inventory is zero. If you can get a good location without selling your plasma, fill your store with good stuff, and promote it well, you can make a success out of your clothing, crafts, furniture, or other consignment store. If you decide to ignore our recommendation to stay away from retail, remember the old adage: the three most important factors for retail success are location, location, and location.

Dating Coach/Matchmaker

We know of only one person who's working as a dating coach, but she's doing okay. Put an ad in the personals section of the paper, offering your services to critique and improve your clients' dating skills. Most of your clients will be men wanting to know how to meet women, start a conversation, and read body language. The next step is to start a dating service, seeing as you have all these trained men on hand. Although the big companies dominate, and there are services for virtually every niche group as well, you might be able to offer matchmaking services to a niche that is not being fully served.

Delivery/Hauling Service

People are lazy. They'll pay you to deliver most anything: candy, firewood, flowers, groceries, meals, parcels, gas, coffee. You can deliver to homes, offices, or gathering places of any kind. Or you can go in the other direction—hauling. Haul away trash, keeping your eyes open for goodies you can possibly recondition and resell.

Genealogy Services

Many people wish they knew more about their family histories. Do the searching, interviews, and research, and write a report of your findings.

Gift Basket Business

Making gift baskets is a competitive business. To stand out you need to personalize your baskets in some way, offer them as part of a gift-buying service, or specialize in one client or basket type.

Handyperson Service

Can you fix anything? Do you like to putter and tinker? Depending on your location, you'll probably have to make it clear that you're unlicensed. But, on the other hand, you're excellent, less expensive than the competition, and can provide glowing testimonials and an unbeatable guarantee. You could also focus on installing skylights, wood stoves, garage doors, or anything else that's theoretically "do-it-yourself" but actually beyond the abilities of the average shmoe.

Mobile Tuneup Service

Establish a route of clients who want you to give their vehicles a regular tuneup. Nothing fancy, just a quick checkup. Your clients won't have to worry about changing the oil, filling the tires with air, or wondering how the spark plugs are sparking. With a big enough route you'll be fairly worry-free as well.

Motivational Speaker

If you're an exciting leader and speak very well, you can make a living, or even a fortune. Start with speaking. Focus your message, perfect your delivery, develop a niche. Then, while your clients are fire-walking, bungee-jumping, and affirming their way to personal power, you can move into writing, publishing, and even infomercials. Hell, it's happened before.

Moving Organizer

Moving is awful. Finding a new home is bad enough without the rest of the ordeal—listening impatiently to the utilities' on-hold messages, carefully packing all the precious treasures, arranging a moving company, filing change-of-address forms. And that doesn't include the final insult of moving into the new place. You'll take the hassle out of the move, organizing it from start to finish for your appreciative, stress-free clients.

Professional Organizer

Find a person, business, or organization in a state of utter disarray. There, that wasn't hard. Now organize them. You've got your color-coded files, your hanging wall charts, and your collection of trays, boxes, containers, and labels, and you know how to use them. And once you get everything in order, you can schedule regular checkups.

Specialized Travel Guide

This occupation is halfway between being a tour guide and a travel agent. You can organize camping or adventure trips to some more-or-less remote place and charge your customers for your organizational and leadership skills. Or you can organize educational trips focused on history, art, language, or politics, complete with teachers if you aren't an expert. How about start-an-import-business trips, where you help clients comb a country for a good import opportunity? Or a pilgrimage to a spiritual place? Or fishing, bicycling, golfing, or stamp-collecting trips?

Sightseeing Guide

If you live in an area that suffers from a significant number of tourists, take advantage and organize sightseeing tours. If you have foreign language skills, focus on groups speaking your language. Network with tourist information offices, hotels, and bed and breakfasts. Unless you live near a major tourist attraction, this may be a seasonal business only.

Window Display Designer

Most owners of retail shops recognize that window displays are extremely important. They also know that their own window displays aren't as good as they ought to be. Your job is to design arresting, attractive—even magnetic—window displays that show products to their best advantage and draw customers in. Try to develop regular clients and, if you live in a sufficiently urban area, think about focusing on one or several store types.

Customizing Your
Perfect Business

YOU'VE DISCOVERED YOUR GUIDING PRINCIPLE, identified your resources, and sifted through the bones of hundreds of business ideas, noting the tasty ones. Now you want to transform at least one of the business ideas you've generated into the blueprint of your perfect business.

Go over the business ideas you've collected thus far. Note all the possible business areas from chapter 3 that aren't *entirely* crazy, and all the businesses in the directory that inspired you to dog-ear this previously unsullied book. Now substitute, combine, limit, enlarge, adapt, and reverse those business ideas. Here's how.

SUBSTITUTE

What groups, services, products, procedures, parts, places, or ingredients can you substitute in the business ideas to create a more powerful idea? How can they become more promotable, beneficial, attractive, safe, or affordable? First break the idea down into its component parts, and then refer to your resources or brainstorm to find suitable substitutes for those parts.

For example, let's say you like something about the idea of making a local-label organic baby food, but it's not totally right for you. What and how can you substitute? First, separate the business into its component parts. We break Organic Baby Food Producer down into organic/baby/food/producer. Also think about what's needed to run a baby food business: the marketing, delivery methods, and so on. Then substitute any of those for something similar from your resources. Your brainstorming might yield:

- anything instead of food that you can distribute to babies (for example, maybe you can start an organic cotton clothing exchange, renting clothes to parents until the baby outgrows them),

- any group other than babies who might want organically prepared food, from diabetics to dieters,

- anything other than baby food that you can produce for the same market (upscale new parents), or

- any market instead of parents who would buy organic baby food (sell as a gift to grandparents and friends, as a baby gift from businesses to workers on parental leave, etc.).

COMBINE

This brainstorming technique is our favorite. You probably have more business ideas than a person could implement in a lifetime. But it's possible that none of them is the perfect expression of your individuality. So pick your favorites, no matter how unrelated, and combine them. Sometimes the results will be silly. But sometimes the act of hooking divergent ideas together will create a terrific new idea. Here's an example. (We just picked it out of the air without any planning to give you an idea of how totally unrelated ideas can be combined.)

Let's say that among your favorite business ideas are Dog Groomer and Furniture Decorator. A three-minute brainstorm to combine all the variations of dog, groomer, furniture, and decorator provides you with:

- decorative dog furniture (doghouses, dog-beds, etc.),

- dog-decorated furniture (chairs with German Shepherd-shaped backs, footrests that look like basset hounds, a line of dalmatian-pattern upholstery),

- self-grooming dog furniture, complete with attached brushes so your dog gets groomed when it enters the doghouse, sleeps in the bed, etc.,

- decorative dog services, in which you dye, shave, attire, or otherwise decorate dogs,

- a paw-casting kit, which allows people to make a plaster cast of their dogs' paws and use them as decorations,

- combined dog-grooming/furniture decorating shop,

- use dog fur you get while grooming to decorate furniture, and

- and, and, and, *aaargh*, our three minutes are up.

Some of these ideas are really dumb. But some have potential, and wouldn't have come up if you hadn't tried combining dissimilar businesses.

In addition to combining ideas to get new services and products, as we did above, you can also combine *ways of doing business*. Many dog groomers make house calls, but few furniture-decorators do so.

We also recommend that you combine your business ideas with any resources you think are particularly valuable. If your best friend's mother is the buyer for a major department store chain, she ought to be included in all your crafty stratagems. If you're a brilliant programmer, you might want to factor that into the equation, even if programming is not your passion.

Limit

Small is beautiful. And niche marketing—aiming at a small target—is one of the most powerful approaches to business success. In fact, it's powerful enough to deserve its own complete section later. Right now, your market is only one of the business attributes you'll try limiting. Also narrow, focus, excise, shrink, streamline, eliminate, or understate your services or product. How can that be a good thing?

Let's say your guiding principle is "I'm a Playful Modifier of Mechanical Things," and one of your favorite business areas is repairing clocks. You can limit the type of service, the kind of clock, or any of the many ways of doing business. For example, you may provide mail-order cuckoo clock repair, or "how to fix your own grandfather clock" instruction. This limits your market, of course—and focuses it.

With products, consider selling smaller, fewer, or limited items. Even the zillion-dollar software companies are selling limited versions of their products, and this is the basis of the huge shareware market. If you're starting a ceramics business, think about selling your products unfinished and letting the buyers decorate them. If you're a small-scale farmer, sell broccoli crowns and individual beets. If you're a musician, offer a half-hour rate.

ENLARGE

Big is also beautiful. Make what you sell larger, add related products or services, add features, give extra value, or offer longer-lasting or more frequent products, services, or promotions.

Diversify. We recommend diversification to every small business. Don't be shallow. Although you can certainly have a primary offer, your business should have more depth than a single product or service. Expand and diversify your business. If you're painting portraits of people's cats, expand into cat greeting cards, portraits of dogs, cat sculpture, a cat-care referral business, whatever. But never be in a situation where you make a sale and then end your relationship with your client. Back-end sales—the sales you make after the first one—are the backbone of almost every successful business. And repeat customers are by far the most valuable people to your business—if you have only one thing to offer, you can't give them a reason to come back for more. If you do nothing else, make sure you have a solid line of products and/or services, not just one single, lonely, dead-end sale.

Larger. What would happen if, instead of making regular-sized ceramic vases, you made them eight to fourteen feet tall? We know of an artist who did just that, and ended up with incredibly distinctive, colossal painted vases that sell for more than many people make in a year. This is also the story behind Magnum condoms. They're 20 percent larger than other brands and offer one of the most irresistible sales pitches of any product in the history of the world.

More Complete. What other related services/products can you offer? If you're offering housecleaning services, you can also include minor repair, paint touch-up, organizational, or safe-home services. Or you can sell the cleaning supplies or other products your clients need to maintain a clean home.

Additional Features. For your housecleaning services, you'd make sure to offer window cleaning as an additional feature. Or you could rent a carpet-cleaning machine a couple of times a year to really get the dirt out, and charge a special fee accordingly. Other expanding features include being longer-lasting or more frequent. Make a cleaning service longer-lasting by taking all day to do the most thorough job possible, or offering a lengthy guarantee of some sort. You could increase the frequency of your services by offering a weekly clutter pick-up service as well.

Extra Value. There's a cleaning service that features topless cleaning. Apparently some lowbrow men are more willing to spend money on a weekly cleaning if there are breasts involved (you'll be relieved to hear that a television exposé—hidden cameras and all—revealed no monkey business, just a nice clean apartment), and don't mind paying a higher heating bill to keep the cleaners warm. You, of course, could just leave a mint on the pillow.

ADAPT

The rude word for adapting is copycatting, but we encourage it nonetheless. Take an existing concept and apply it to your business or give it a new twist and make it your own. You know those silhouette-of-a-naked-woman whoodingies that you see on the mudflaps of semis and pickup trucks? Adapt that. Make a silhouette of a naked man, a goddess figurine, a woman with a rocket launcher, whatever. Or take a simple idea like subscriptions and apply it to a business that's not commonly subscribed to. That's how Community Supported Agriculture (see description in chapter 15) was born, and you could do the same with many other service or product businesses.

Whenever you see a business strategy, marketing method, or plain old good idea, be alert for potential adaptation possibilities. Be aware of what you buy and why, and what makes you feel satisfied with a product or service. Also think of any business that you're particularly loyal to, that is substantially more successful than similar businesses, or that does well despite your expectations. And don't disregard ideas that come from outside the business sphere—look for profitable, reproducible ideas everywhere.

REVERSE

You can also generate or modify your business ideas by being contrary. You could think about how to defy expectations, reverse roles, buck a trend, and move backwards. Let's say you're thinking of offering a genealogical service. People love to know about all their wonderful forebears. Can you specialize in finding the rotten apple on the family tree? Perhaps you could write about criminal insanity in famous families.

Or you can defy a trend and spit in the face of progress. There is always that small group of people who prefer the old way of doing things, no matter what those things are—and that small group is usually big enough to support a trend-defying business or two. Sell and service manual typewriters (which are fast becoming valuable as antiques as well as office machines), manufacture MSG, or start a crusade against the Internet.

Role reversal includes reversing actual roles as well as reversing those stereotypical, expected roles. Restaurants get much mileage from actual role reversal. Both delivery, where the food goes to the clients' house, and salad bars, where the customers serve themselves, are examples of role reversal. If you're a florist, you get paid to make flower arrangements at weddings, right? Well, maybe you can just supply the flowers and let the bridal party make the arrangements as a pre-wedding event.

Reversing actual stereotypes can also be a rewarding source of ideas. Think of a stereotype of one of the groups or products that you listed in your resources. For instance, it's usually assumed, rightly or wrongly, that women don't like drinking beer, men don't like buying shoes, loggers hate spotted owls, actors are flaky. Then reverse the stereotype and see if you get anything interesting: women's beer, a catalog for shoe-obsessed men, "Hug-an-Owl" T-shirts for loggers, contact management software for actors.

Not only does being contrary come naturally, but it can boost your business as well.

PUTTING IT ALL TOGETHER

But just reading about ways to customize your business ideas doesn't do much. You've got to force the idea into a new shape. Write down your favorite ideas on the following chart, and have your way with them. We suggest that you customize your business ideas using each of the six variations.

Business Idea	Customization	Creation (New Business Idea)
Gourmet dessert business	Substitute	Gourmet breakfasts
	Combine	Gourmet cat treats
	Limit	Eclairs
	Enlarge	Gourmet meals
	Adapt	Low-fat eclairs
	Reverse	Desserts as appetizers
	Substitute	
	Combine	
	Limit	
	Enlarge	
	Adapt	
	Reverse	
	Substitute	
	Combine	
	Limit	
	Enlarge	
	Adapt	
	Reverse	
	Substitute	
	Combine	
	Limit	
	Enlarge	
	Adapt	
	Reverse	
	Substitute	
	Combine	
	Limit	
	Enlarge	
	Adapt	
	Reverse	

GOING MODULAR

Many traditional small business books tell you that you have to work eighteen hours a day, six days a week if you want to be a success. Quit the bowling league, send the kids to boarding school, and kiss your life goodbye. Then they say that you'll love every minute of it, because you're the boss. Well, we don't know about you, but there's *nothing* that we want to do for eighteen hours a day no matter how much we enjoy it. No, nothing.

And that's OK, because you can start modular businesses. We've already discussed expanding your business into related areas, but this is one step beyond that. Let's say you want to start two unrelated businesses. Or even three or four. Here's the trick: Do it.

Oh, you can't start them all at once. That's beyond even your amazing powers of entrepreneurial wizardry. To borrow a metaphor from Barbara Winter, author of *Making a Living without a Job*, you'll be like one of those jugglers who spins plates on top of sticks. You get one going first, spinning merrily away. When it no longer needs your constant centrifugal supervision, you start whacking at another plate. When that one is up to speed, move on. After you've got them all going, they still need some spin control, but not full-time micro-management. Some of them *will* fly out of control and shatter on the floor. That's a pity—it was such a nice plate—but it's not a disaster. You've still got a bunch of healthy spinners.

The Leap

Do you keep your job while starting your business, or do you burn your bridges?

We've done both. As responsible author-types, we recommend working at least part-time while you're starting your business, unless you've got a trust fund or some other source of income. Steady income, even if the result of deadly work, has a certain calming effect on the spirit. On the other hand, if you can live off of dust bunnies and free rent at a parent's or friend's house, have enough money to run your business and your life for about four months, and are chomping at the bit, take the leap. You can always go crawling to a temp agency looking for work to fill in the gaps.

Maybe you can understand why you'd expand a business into related areas, but you don't follow the modular business plan. Why would you want to scatter your energy by starting a bunch of unrelated enterprises? Won't they all be pitifully undernourished and starved for your attention? Well, if it makes you *that* uncomfortable, fine. Suit yourself.

In fact, many business startup guru types would be aghast at our modular business recommendation because they insist that you focus with laser-like intensity on one task until you succeed. That's great if you're able to work yourself up to that sort of commitment, and if you want to make heaps of money. If you'd rather have a great time, and build a good adequate income, it's not necessary.

But going modular does offer some attractive benefits:

- Less vulnerability to business cycles provides you with a more stable income. All businesses go through up times and down times. When you lose a couple of your personal chef customers to food poisoning, you'll be pretty pleased with those book indexing projects you just got.

- It's easier to make $800 a month from three businesses than it is to make $2,400 from one. You may design four window displays a month at $200 a pop, organize eight homes for $100 each, and have 100 businesses subscribing to your "How to Make Maximum Money from Your Coffee Shop" newsletter at $96 per year.

- You won't get bored. Even if you're running a business you love, the chances are that there will be things you don't like about it, or you'll occasionally get just a wee bit tired of indulging your passion again and again. Not so if you've got some diversity in your business life.

- Cross-pollination: Ideas, experience, and contacts from one business will help you in the others. Remember, though, that your businesses are separate entities. They each deserve their own name, business cards, and marketing plan, etc. If you're passing out brochures that say "Happy Pumpkin Services: Aura Cleansing, Fund-raising, and Nutritional Consulting," we guarantee you'll get plenty of business from that one person who wants all three services, and virtually none from the masses, which want only one.

If you eat your salad in alphabetical order ("Ohmigod, I ate the arti-choke before the watercress!") and you get mad that the dressing is all over everything instead of staying neatly between the croutons and the endive, starting modular businesses might not work for you. That's fine. Focus on diversifying your business in related areas.

You might think that we're encouraging contradictory behavior—specializing and diversifying—but you *can* do both simultaneously. Each one of your diverse efforts will be narrowly targeted. Don't start a sec-retarial service for businesses, a bookkeeping service for businesses, and a referral service for businesses. Start a secretarial service for realtors, a bookkeeping service for graphic designers (or realtors), and a referral ser-vice for children's services (or graphic designers/realtors). Ta da!—you've got a trio of diverse, targeted businesses.

By this time, you have one or several cunning business ideas that are virtually guaranteed to rocket you to riches. But now that you've combined, adapted, limited, and otherwise transmogrified your business ideas, it's time for us to let you in on a little secret. It's impossible to start a successful business based entirely on a great idea, even the incred-ible ideas you've been generating thanks to this book. You need more than ideas. You need CUSTOMERS.

From Passion to Profit: Make Your Business a Money-Magnet

PART THREE

Reducing the Risks—
Finding Customers
Before Startup

IF YOU START A BUSINESS you dislike but customers love, you'll become rich and unsatisfied. But if you start a business you love and customers hate, you'll be bankrupt and as satisfied as a diva who only sings in the shower. We don't care how much of an iron-willed artiste or visionary loner you are—when you start a business only you can love, the results are painful.

> "If you can build a better mousetrap, the world will beat a path to your door." Bullshit! Great ideas and better products or services never guarantee success. Not until you persuasively present them to an accessible market of soon-to-be-satisfied customers are you headed toward success. It is the constant lament of half-assed entrepreneurs that other businesses do better than theirs, despite offering lower quality. Well, the competitors' quality *is* much higher—because they actually serve the customers. They've identified their market and promoted the benefits of their product or service with entrepreneurial savvy. That's a higher-quality business than one that would produce better results if the customers only knew they existed.

What you need is accessible customers who need, want, and can afford your products or services. And the only way to determine if you have them is through market research.

Usually, market research starts with customers' needs. That makes a whole lot of sense—the only real foundation a small business ever has is a mess of needy customers. But you don't just want people who need what you're selling. You want customers to whom you can sell. If you've got a great idea but, after months of brainstorming, research, and prayer, you've finally admitted the only way to promote it is by convincing David Duke, Andrea Dworkin, Nancy Reagan, and Louis Farrakhan to work together at your wig factory, you haven't got a great idea. You've got a sick fantasy.

ACCESSIBLE CUSTOMERS

If you're starting a newsletter for reclusive misanthropes that is full of useful tips about avoiding and despising people, and offered at an affordable price, you're still sunk. Why? Because reclusive misanthropes are an inaccessible market. They don't go to conventions, sign up for mailing lists, or read *Reclusive Misanthrope Today* magazine.

Well, that's pretty straightforward, and the markets you already have in mind are probably not "Congresspeople Committing Adultery" or "People Wanted by the Law." But there is another approach to developing a rewarding market:

> *Identify a market to which you have better-than-average access. Then customize your product or service to fit that market. This is a good example of reversal—instead of developing a product or service and then figuring out how to market it, you find a marketing channel and then develop an appropriate offering. It's backwards and it might not work for your circumstances, but give it a try. If you can make it happen, you'll be amply rewarded.*

Sure, but how?

You've still got your resource maps, haven't you? Go through them—especially your People Map—and note any that provide a means to communicate with a possible market.

- Do you have resources that provide access to a mass market? Include any contacts who are in, or have contacts in, radio, television, magazines, newspapers, or other mass media. The Internet offers easy access, of course, but it's probably the least valuable, too. And the media aren't the only way to reach masses of people. If you know the Acting Assistant Associate Vice President of Toys 'R' Us, that's a possible connection to a mass market.

- Do you have a resource that provides access to a limited market? Can you communicate through clubs, associations, schools, organizations, and religious groups? Do you know the treasurer of the National Rock-Climbing Association? The president of the North American Jackie Chan Fan Club? Although these may or may not provide a long-term market, don't worry about that right now—both examples could jump-start any number of businesses.

- Do you have a contact, or any other resource, who has any degree of national celebrity? Do you know someone who knows someone who knows someone who does? Not just Hollywood-type celebrities, but nationally-known experts in less glamorous fields, too.

- Then think of local celebrities: do you know the best-known artist in town? The most popular psychic? The most successful realtor? Who do they have access to?

- Do you know people who can't shut up? Can you wind them up and send them off, chattering about your business all the while? What sort of people, groups, and situations do they have access to? Or do you know someone who knows everyone in her field or interest group?

- Can you convert your stuff into access to people? Do you have a pet who always attracts attention? A vehicle that gathers a crowd? What sorts of people are interested?

- Can you convert your skills into access? Do people cluster round when you whittle? Are they enthralled while watching your dynamic cooking style? Who clusters, who's enthralled?

- Are you part of a group that could be a valuable market? Do you have contacts who are?

Pick the most promising or interesting contacts, stuff, or skills. Let's say you have a friend who TAs a massive lecture class at a local university, your homemade hats always get favorable attention when you walk around wearing one, and your aunt does Julia Child's hair. Can you connect any of your business ideas to these ready-made marketing opportunities?

Would any of your ideas be jump-started by being presented to hundreds of captive college students per semester? How can you transform people's admiration of your hats into a sale for one of your businesses (and it doesn't even have to be a hat business)? Can you develop one of your ideas into a product or service that would benefit from Julia Child's recommendation?

If you don't find a convenient on-ramp onto the commercial freeway lurking in your resources, that's fine. You might not have the contacts, or the ones you have might not be appropriate to any of your businesses. After reading this marketing section, you'll know how to grab most markets by the throat and shake until they cough up cash. But access to local celebrities, gatekeepers of the special-interest media, and religious, ethnic, and other groups is more common than you might think. And because you're probably going to start a local or special-interest business, these resources can be extremely rewarding.

So, if you can, customize your idea to fit the accessible market. As long as you still find the work satisfying, don't worry if it leads one of your brilliant ideas down a slightly odd path. You've got to become a big fish in a muddy puddle before you move on to the small pond. And you can still develop additional markets and additional marketing strategies later, when you work on diversifying your business.

NEEDS

We're obliged to include at least one quote from Peter Drucker, business guru extraordinaire. Here it is, from Drucker's book *Management: Tasks and Responsibilities*:

> *True marketing starts...with the customer...It does not ask, "What do we want to sell?" It asks, "What does the customer want to buy?" It does not say, "This is what our product or service does." It says, "These are the satisfactions the customer looks for, values, and needs...The aim of marketing is to know and understand the customer so well that the product or service fits him {or her} and sells itself."*

Even if you have an accessible market, a great sales campaign, a useful product or service, and floss daily, your business won't succeed unless it's meeting your customers' needs. This is the basis of market research—what does your market need? The most powerful needs tend to be the

A Tale

There's a famous (well, if you're a small-business geek) story about a company that found success almost entirely due to the accessible market it approached.

There was once a young man who wanted to make a fortune in direct mail. He tried selling one thing; it failed. He tried selling another; it failed. He tried selling something else; it failed, too. He was out of money, living in a cave, eating dirt.

He knew that for a direct mail campaign to work, he had to have a good mailing list. But our hero had checked his resources for an accessible market, and hadn't found one. Then, with a vision born of desperation, he realized he had a great resource he hadn't considered before: the phone book. But what good is a phone book? It doesn't have any information about the people listed. It doesn't tell you if they like kites, buy books through the mail, or are golfers. It just lists names.

Then came his inspiration. See if you can figure it out for yourself. If all you have is a list of names and addresses, what can you sell? You can't sell something everyone uses—like soap or toilet paper. No, you need to develop a product or service aimed at a niche market. But all you have is a list of names and addresses. How can you *customize a business idea to fit the accessible market*—people with certain names and addresses.

Give up? You sell a "family crest research report." You target some common names, research their family crests, and mail it to people with that name. But how successful was it? Well, as of now about 100 million of those letters have been mailed, generating more than 7.5 million orders. And the company has diversified into related areas—family crests on plaques, clothing, and giftware. It currently sells to more than a million customers a year.

That's pretty good for a business that started in a cave. And it's all because of the focus on *providing an appropriate (and unique) service or product to an accessible market.*

most fundamental: money, success, power, pleasure, love, beauty, sex, friends, fun, health, and so on. Cater to them and you will be rewarded.

WANTS

The reason we talk about customers' needs *and* wants is because it's possible to find a prospective customer who needs what you're selling but doesn't want it, or who wants what you're selling but doesn't need it. When you're doing market research and you discover that people need what you've got but they don't want it, assume that they will never become customers.

You'll be tempted to hurl them to the ground, step on their throats, and explain very clearly why it would be obvious to a half-witted sheep that they need what you're selling. Resist the urge. The best thing that can happen is you'll finally convince them to buy: they'll feel manipulated (for good reason), and you'll have wasted much time and more energy on a client who'll probably never buy from you again.

So customers must both need and want what you're selling.

AND CAN AFFORD

This is pretty simple. If customers can't afford to pay you—and you can't dream up an alternative way of transferring the appropriate amount of their wealth to you—it doesn't much matter how much they need and want your product or service. They just can't have it (leaving aside the bit of pro bono work you'll do).

If you're creative enough, though, and your prospective customer wants to pay you enough, you probably can dream up an alternative payment scheme. Payment and installment plans and bartering are the two most obvious examples, and you can develop any number of innovative variations on them.

MARKET RESEARCH

Fine. You need to determine what your customers want, need, and can afford *before* starting your business. But how? Market research. The problem is that, on a tiny entrepreneurial scale, market research can cost more than actually starting a business. Corporate juggernauts spend tremendous amounts of money on market research, and then do something like release New Coke. But if you're going to make a huge error of judgment when starting your business, you've got to do it on a very tight budget. And despite the fact that small-scale market research will rarely tell you with complete accuracy if you have a sure-fire winner, it's good at knocking you down, bouncing your head off the pavement, kicking you in the side, and telling you that you have a sure-fire stinker.

But although it can be the bearer of ill tidings and a wee bit tedious, and may even delay your triumphal grand opening, you've just got to do your research.

We're ashamed to admit that we started a business without market research. We began a mail order company with an artist friend, selling very cool T-shirts to skaters, slackers, and other kids with bad manners. Our market research consisted of saying, "Ooooh, groovy," checking magazines to see if there were any T-shirt ads, and wandering around local skate shops looking as old as Mick Jagger at a Foo Fighters concert. Although that particular business was crippled by our naiveté (read: idiocy), it might have been salvaged or put out of its misery before we spent money on ads, by some not-so-difficult market research.

Market research starts with questions. The bottom-line question is always, "Are there enough accessible customers who want, need, and can afford my products or services to support my business?" But that's not an effective research question. *These* are effective research questions:

- What markets do I have access to?

- Who are the members of those markets? What are they like? What do they do, wear, eat, hate, read, etc.?

- Is my target group big enough to support my business?

- Are there businesses offering similar services or products? Who are their customers? How do they get 'em? How well do they do with their finances, quality, repeat business, etc.?

- Are there businesses offering different services or products to my target market? What, how, and how well do they do?

- What needs does my business meet? What are the benefits to the customers?

- How can I meet more needs or meet needs better? How can I change my offering to suit this target market?

- What other target markets need this product or service? What related products or services does this target market need?

- How often do prospective customers buy similar goods or services, and how much do they spend?

- What will they pay for my products or services?

Customer Profile

You won't know who your customers will be before you start your business. But you can guess. Picture a representative customer. Describe his or her:

Sex: _____

Age: _____

Race/Ethnicity/Religion: _____

Class/Income: _____

Occupation:_____

Hobbies/Interests: _____

Lifestyle: _____

Educational level: _____

Other important characteristics: _____

Primary benefit(s) they get from your business:

Once you're in business, check your assumptions to see if they're true. You might be surprised to discover that the thong underwear you sell is being bought by little kids to use as slingshots. Also use the profile to inspire appropriate marketing strategies. What does this person read or watch? How can you appeal to this person's needs and explain the primary benefit of buying your product or service?

If your customers are businesses instead of individuals, you still have to make a customer profile. Describe their size, products or services, location, interests, and so on.

That might look like an overwhelming number of questions. You don't need to ask them all, but do find the ones you think are most appropriate. Make sure you know who your customers are, what they spend on similar products or services, and how to reach them.

If you're thinking of starting a business as a college application essay coach, you might ask: Who's my market—college-bound students or their parents? How many of them are out there? Will they pay for my essay hand-holding? How much? What other services or products do they need? What do they see as the benefits of my service?

Then you need some answers.

MARKET RESEARCH TECHNIQUES

There are two kinds of market research data: primary, which you get yourself, and secondary, which is already out there. The big differences are these: gathering primary data costs money, if only the amount of a long-distance phone call. Secondary data is often free in census reports, surveys, and news articles. Primary data is usually useful. Secondary data is usually less so.

Secondary Research

The problem with secondary data is that, for example, if you're starting an essay coaching business, it doesn't help you all that much to know that 1.48 million high school students enroll in college per year, the average income of the family of a college applicant is $30,820, and 79 percent of high school seniors can't write their names without moving their lips. Oh, it helps a little—if the average income were $822.09 and 79 percent of high school seniors were brilliant writers, you'd probably decide to start another business instead. And if there were 27 million of them, with an average family income of $234,000, you'd be forgiven for whistling a jaunty little tune and skipping a bit. But it's more likely that it won't be very helpful. Why not? It's too broad. You're not marketing to college applicants or their families. You're marketing to the parents of college applicants in Correctionville, Minnesota who are members of the PTA, because you're using the PTA mailing list.

But secondary research can be useful. Besides the broader sources of secondary research, such as demographic statistics, media surveys and polls, and scientific studies, there's also more practical, targeted information: competitors' catalogs and price sheets, back issues of magazines and newsletters chock full of ads for similar businesses, and the Yellow Pages and other directories. Which brings us to...

The Ultimate Secondary Research Resource: Reference Librarians

If you want to discover statistics, census data, or whatever that's related to your putative business, ask a reference librarian to point you in the right direction. In fact, just about twenty minutes ago, when we were making up those statistics for the essay coaching business, we thought we'd conduct a little experiment. We called the reference desk at the local library and asked how many high school students enroll in college per year. In two minutes, the librarian told us that the most recent statistics she could find indicated 2,398,000 high school grads, 61.7 percent of whom enrolled in college. If our math is right, that's about 1.48 million new college students. The rest of those statistics are bogus, but it took us less than five minutes to get that one real number. And it cost us nothing. Reference librarians are gods. If you get stuck, prostrate yourself before one and intone, "Uhhh. Could you help me?"

This works for product development research as well. If you're looking for a private label manufacturer of pillows, ask the reference librarian where to find one. We'd mention our favorite directories, but that would be distressingly like an elementary school "How to Use Your Public Library" class, and the librarians do it so much better in any case.

Other sources of secondary research are local business development centers, SCORE (Service Corps of Retired Executives, a wonderful group, though often oriented to larger small businesses), your local Chamber of Commerce, and computer databases.

We once went to a self-help, goal-setting seminar at which the speaker said, "If you get nothing else from this class, remember one thing: the most powerful technique you can use to get what you want is to *GET SOME EXPERT ADVICE*." And you know what? We can't remember anything else, but it was still well worth the admission fee.

The majority of people, especially the ones you most want to speak with—reputable, generous, knowledgeable—are very happy to help if they're approached nicely. It's flattering to be asked for advice. If you can ask a question and then keep your mouth shut until the answer is complete, you've got an almost unfair business advantage.

And don't just ask "certified" experts. Ask anyone who can do something you can't, which is everyone. Just ask. Ask, ask, ask. Ask. And then ask some more.

Although secondary research won't tell you if your customers are likely to buy, it can let you know if you're in the ballpark, provide you with leads, and help you refine your primary research.

Primary Research, or The Truth Is Out There

Primary research is when you assemble your own data, either from undigested sources such as the phone book or by actually asking people questions. The library is a great place to start your primary research. Snoop around. Flip through the telephone and other directories to see if there's a need for your business. (You might want to focus on the Standard Rate and Data books to learn about magazines and mailing lists that target your market.) Check for competition and related businesses, and don't worry if you find some. A little competition is a good thing— it indicates a need for your business. But if you'll be the first, that either means that you're on the cutting edge, or under it—and you can't tell which until you do primary research.

Find out about your competitors' pricing, and the benefits they stress in their marketing materials. Look for information about your clients—if they are businesses, find out what their market is, and what benefits *they* stress. That way, if you find that all the house painters in your town mention the speed of their service in their advertisements, you know that's a concern. Then you can tell them "Speed is essential for house painters. I can help you improve your turnaround."

You can do much of the same research in stores, as well. Find a similar product and see how it's packaged, promoted, and priced. If it's a nice, small store, you can even get some expert advice: tell the owner or manager that you're thinking of starting a business producing a similar product, and ask if they like your idea, and what they like and dislike about their current product. Then listen.

But you still haven't directly contacted your prospective customers. You have all those questions you generated and few answers. It's time to get your hands dirty, with chatting, questionnaires and surveys, the Internet, and focus groups.

Chatting:

This is informal—or we should say qualitative, not quantitative—market research. Talk to salespeople and customers at related businesses, businesspeople in networking groups, and members of all sorts of associations applicable to your business. Know what questions you want answered, and lead conversations in that direction. This isn't as rigorous as a survey, but can result in more valuable information. Instead of rating your menu planning services on a scale of 1 to 10, someone might casually mention that he's been helped by incorporating a menu planner into his daily organizer, giving you new ideas and unselfconscious advice.

Questionnaires and Surveys:

There's a very scientific approach to questionnaires and surveys, which rigorously takes into account wording, question order, sample size, and so on. But you can't afford such luxuries. Instead, you're faced with three questions: Who will you ask? How will you ask? What will you ask?

Who and how will you ask? You've got a target market and a customer profile. That's who you'll ask. Try to approach them for your survey or questionnaire in the same way you're planning on approaching them for their business. If you're planning to rely heavily on direct-mail, mail a questionnaire. If you're going to be relying on referrals, ask for referrals to people who'd answer a questionnaire. If you'll be doing telemarketing, phone. If you'll be selling directly to people at a local craft show, go talk to them. If you're intending to get clients through advertising, advertise for them (this includes everything from posting flyers to magazine advertising).

What will you ask? There are many ways to ask questionnaire questions. The most common are using open-ended questions, yes-or-no or multiple choice questions, or ranking questions. Because you're working with a very small sample, you probably want to use a good number of open-ended or narrative response questions. Your results won't be statistically significant in any case, so you might as well get as much information as you can. The exception is when speed and ease are important. People are more willing to answer "no" or "three" or "b" than to have to really think about your question.

The kind of questions you ask also depends in part on how you're distributing the survey. In-person or phone surveys lend themselves to open-ended questions. Mail and drop-off surveys that you leave behind in appropriate places work better with multiple choice or ranking questions.

Then you've got to decide on wording. You know enough not to ask: "Would Competitor X's inefficiency, ignorance, and bad breath lead you to want to work with a different service provider?" But also stay away from: "Would you pay more for higher quality?" or "On a scale of 1 to 10, how would you rate the importance of buying a non-toxic, earth-friendly product even if it cost a bit more?" Who's going to say no, they'd prefer lower quality at a lower price, or that they couldn't care less about the environment? It can be difficult to avoid value judgments entirely, but do your best: "Would you pay $179.95 for a pair of custom-fitted, hand-made hiking boots?" "Would a guarantee persuade you to buy the boots? If so, what length? a) six months, b) one year, c) two years, d) three years or 3,000 miles, or e) lifetime."

Internet

The cool thing about doing market research on the Internet is that it's free. The downside is that it hasn't been done enough for anyone to know how well it works. We think it makes good sense that online market research works if you're researching an online business. And it may work as a convenient way to contact people who match your customer profile. If you'll be selling to people who oppose the death penalty, for example, there's a newsgroup on that very topic. In addition to being free, an e-mail survey or newsgroup posting has the added benefit of getting a good, nearly instantaneous, response. E-mail is perceived as being both more intimate than regular mail and less intrusive than a phone call, which makes it ideal for market research.

To find online survey fodder:

- Ask questions on appropriate newsgroups.

- E-mail your survey to people who participate in newsgroup discussions.

- Use commercial online services and BBSs. Ask your questions in forums, message centers, or whatever your service calls them. We use America Online, despite the abuse. AOL is the lowest-status online address—which, perversely, is another reason we use it. We think it's worth using for two reasons: it has six million subscribers as of this writing, and it has a searchable directory of members, where many subscribers list their occupation, hobbies, and so forth. We searched for "Jackie Chan" and found eighty-two members who mentioned him in their member profiles, and found seventeen Colorado-based astrologers listed under "Astrologer and CO." Not enough for a scientific sample, perhaps, but you can get some valuable feedback.

- The Web can be used this same way, as a searchable directory of people who list their interests, hobbies, and occupations. The Web is huge, so you can get a bigger sample than you would on AOL. Use one of the many search engines to find your victims, check out their homepages, and ask away.

We recommend doing at least a cursory Internet survey if you're already online. If you're not online, don't bother: you've got enough to worry about in the real world. But as far as easy, free, and painless market research goes, the Internet stands alone. And listen to what people say. We've been dissuaded from starting two businesses based on Internet-generated research results.

Focus Group

You can use focus groups (which, despite the name, are nothing more than a bunch of people sitting around a table waiting until they can get at the donuts) for feedback on your product, service, offer, advertising, or anything else that you'll be presenting to the public. Feed them your new line of muffins, have them paw over your fabric samples, ask them any of your survey questions, and listen to the resulting opinions.

Of course, focus groups are usually paid. If your friends are your target group, you can probably get by with a couple of pizzas. Otherwise, be prepared to offer creative remuneration or part with a bit of cash.

Be creative—there are as many ways to elicit feedback from a target market as there are target markets. Focus on what your market would respond to, what they'd respond for, and what they'd respond with, and custom-design a market research technique aimed at discovering the innermost workings of their buy/don't buy decision-making.

Testing

If you have several products or services, you can test them against each other. This gives you more objective feedback, and it doesn't have to be expensive. Plus you can usually test an idea without having a prototype or an established service. You test by offering your prospective customers, through whatever marketing channel you plan on using, a free product or service in exchange for telling you which product is their favorite.

You can test through direct mail or networking or publicity, or any other marketing technique. Here's an example for telephone testing:

"Hi. I'm calling from (YourBizName). Would you like to participate in a short marketing survey for three new products (or services)? For participating, you could get one of these products free (or for fifty percent off or whatever)."

If they say no, fine. Dial the next number. If they say yes, or ask what you're talking about, tell them that you're trying to determine which of three products or services to market. Tell them that you're going to read short descriptions of each product or service, and will then ask them to choose the one they'd like to have, if any. Tell them that if they choose the one you decide to market, they'll get it for free (fifty percent off, etc.) when it becomes available, for participating in the survey.

Sales Simulation

If you're obsessive and really want to see your respondents in a buying situation, you'll have to part with some money. This works best in a focus group, where you can be sure you've identified your target market and you have your group's complete attention. But you can do it through any of your possible marketing channels. What you do is simple:

- Present your sales pitch. Make it as similar as possible to the pitch you'll use to actually make sales (so if you'll be selling through direct mail, don't show the actual product, just the sales letter you'd send).

- If you have several proposed products or services, present each one.

- Have group members rate the product(s) or service(s) and give feedback.

- Give them sufficient cash to buy one of the products or services. Yes, actual cash.

- Tell them they can buy the product(s) or service(s) with the cash, or just keep it.

If they're your target market, they've heard your pitch, and you've given them money to buy your product or service, *and they still don't buy it,* you're in trouble. Now we don't expect all of them to buy it, but you should expect a better response than you'd get in the real-life market.

There is no better way to discover how people will act in the marketplace than a sales simulation, except for, well, contacting people in the marketplace. If you're impulsive, overconfident, and bull-headed, you may blow off any of the above market research techniques. But do not disregard the power of...

STARTING SMALL

When we started our financial aid consulting business, two of our market research techniques were sending a press release to the local weekly paper to see if it got printed and generated phone calls, and calling high school guidance counselors to see if they liked the idea of our business and would refer us to students' families.

The press release was printed, and the guidance counselors were fairly encouraging. At that point, the only thing we'd invested in the business was time and the cost of materials to learn how to run the business. We used public relations and networking as cornerstones of our marketing strategy, to check the local level of interest in our business. If no one had responded to the article, and none of the guidance counselors had referred us to families, we'd probably have done a small direct mail test and then, if that failed, modified our offer or given up. As it was, our phone started ringing, and the guidance counselors referred us to several families. We were off and running, with the minimal market research transformed into the foundation of our marketing campaign.

You can do the same with most businesses. Test the current. Put your toe in. Then your foot, up to your ankle. *Then* jump in. Don't do your market research and then invest three months and the maximum cash advance on your credit card making fused glass napkin holders before trying to make a sale. Incorporate sales into your market research. Make some samples of your napkin holder. Rent a corner of someone else's booth at a craft show and talk to buyers for kitchen supply stores. Speak to craft stores until one or two of them mention the possibility of selling your napkin holders on consignment. If buyers give you positive feedback, send thank-you notes, keep in touch until you're ready to roll out your product on a grand scale, and then exploit them for all they're worth. By starting small, you're doing research and creating selling opportunities at the same time.

You're rewarded for doing the only thing you can afford to do— growing your business organically. You plant a seed here, and tend it. You plant a seed there. You just tend your small patch. And if you're not planting in rocky soil, it grows. You may learn that although your soil doesn't do much for beefsteak tomatoes, once you change to jetstar tomatoes you've got something. Or maybe all tomatoes wither on the vine, while corn flourishes. Or maybe we ought to stop this paragraph before we metaphor again.

You get the picture. Starting small isn't only a necessity. It's also a blessing.

All the market research techniques we discuss can be combined with free samples and special offers for best results. Samples and offers give you three benefits:

- they increase the research response (people are always more willing to do something for something than something for nothing),

- they are themselves a form of market research—if people aren't interested in getting your product for free just for speaking with you on the phone for three minutes, that's valuable feedback, and

- they create a core of people who have used your services/products, and can be mined for testimonials, referrals, and repeat business.

Planning on Success

YOU'VE GOT A LEAN, mean business idea that complements your guiding principle and satisfies the needs of your prospective customers. But now, as if you haven't done enough already, you've got to get down to the details. It's time to write your business plan.

Many small-time startups don't bother to write a business plan. They figure they don't need one: they won't get bank financing anyway, and they can manage the nitty-gritty without writing it down. Their business is nothing complex—it's just them, selling copywriting services or whatever. Well, they're right and wrong. If they're anything like us, they won't get bank financing. The old adage about banks not lending money to anyone who needs to borrow money is true. And maybe they *can* keep most of the day-to-day details in their heads. But there are still five reasons to write a business plan:

- **Financial feedback.** You might find that given your overhead, the maximum price you can charge for a product or service, and the minimum cost of a product or service, you cannot make money. At this point you can tweak the business or you can discard it as fundamentally flawed. Or you might find that you're right on track, aimed straight at global fame and fortune.

- **Improvement.** As you write your plan, you'll find yourself filling in holes, expanding on strategies, and developing new ideas. You can also tinker: see what happens if you sell fewer items at a higher markup or rent an office instead of working out of your apartment.

- **Confidence.** Once you write your plan down, it begins to make sense. You look at it and—if the numbers work—you think, "Look at that. A business." It's not just a fantasy, it's the seed of a thriving enterprise. You begin to suspect you're not just a scheming nebbish, but a proper small-time entrepreneur.

- **Direction and priority.** Instead of running around dealing with crises as they emerge, or randomly working on whatever you *think* is important, you have a game plan. You know that you've got to do this month's marketing in order to get next month's business, that you have to find a more affordable supplier, and that you can't offer an additional 15 percent discount, because then you'd be losing money. You know what you're aiming at and how you intend to get there.

- **Motivation.** The plan gets you out the door. No matter how detailed it is, it won't accurately predict the growth of your business. In fact, within a month of starting, you'll find that most of the assumptions in your plan are wrong. But you need a solid, steady, rational starting-point from which to fling yourself into the chaos of small-business ownership. That's your plan: a jumping-off point.

You'll notice that financing, which is, after all, the most common reason for writing a business plan, didn't make it onto our list. That doesn't mean that raising a couple of bucks is a bad thing though, or that a business plan can't help raise money. For bigger startups, a business plan is an indispensable fund-raising tool. But *you* have different financing possibilities and priorities.

FINANCING

One of the problems with financing is that it becomes an end in itself, or an excuse—"If only I could raise $35,000, I could start this great business." But the goal is not to get financing. It's to build a thriving business. You can do that with very little money. Ask yourself what you really need to start up. What *must* you spend money on? How can you cut costs? How small can you start? All of these questions lead you to a manageable startup oriented toward the fundamentals, the foundation of any future success you'll have. And having said that....

It's possible that you're some sort of freak who can qualify for a bank loan. If that's the case you'll need a more formal, painful business plan than you'll get from this book. There are many good books available on writing a business plan that will help you get financing. But even if you have a glow-in-the-dark credit rating and managed a similar business for five years, banks are reluctant to lend small amounts of money. They do the same amount of work for a $7,000 business loan that they do for a $70,000 one, and they make a lot more interest off the larger amount. Well, you know we recommend starting slow, but if the Big Bang is your style, knock yourself out.

Otherwise, you basically have two financing options: yourself, and your friends and family. If you've got savings, credit, stuff you can sell, or expendable expenses, you can use that money to start a business. We've started a business with help from all of these.

A note on cash advances from credit cards

We've done it. The attraction is that getting the money is easy. And if you don't pay it back, you just declare bankruptcy and you don't alienate friends or family. But with twentysomething-percent interest rates, it's extremely costly. Factor card payments into your financial figures and see if that doesn't motivate you to find money somewhere else.

If you have no savings, credit, stuff, or unnecessary expenses, start mooching from friends and family.

Borrowing money from them can be tricky, though. You know your friends and family better than we do, but it's a fact that not a few relationships have been ripped asunder because of a business involvement. First, decide who to hit up for money by asking yourself who *you'd* lend money to. And then have everything in writing. This isn't only for legal reasons, but for reasons of clarity—if you lose your best friend because you couldn't pay back $500, that's bad. If you lose your best friend because of a stupid misunderstanding that could've been resolved by writing everything down, that's even worse. Make sure everyone knows that whatever money they give you could go up in smoke, be very aware of emotional strings, and ensure that if you go belly-up you won't be dragging anyone else down with you.

You can borrow more than money. Borrow time by asking people to help out for free when your business is at an awkward growth stage. Borrow computer equipment, furniture, an extra room for storage or an office, or even a fashionable address. *Always, always* borrow expertise. Your contacts have much more to offer you than simple cash—just ask them for it.

You can also borrow someone's good name, through co-signing. It can be a pretty attractive way to get a loan. You have nothing but a sure-fire business plan. Your folks have nothing but a house. If they co-sign your loan using their home as collateral, you'll get the cash to launch your doggy ear wax removal product. Everything's fine so far. But in a year, when your parents have to move into your apartment with you, things might be a tad unhappy. Co-signing works great if the risk is acceptable and the relationship is close. Otherwise, beware.

Even though you're not writing your business plan for sneering bank managers, make sure that it's literate and complete. If you're borrowing money from your parents or an ergonomic chair from a cousin or two hours of envelope stuffing from a friend, you ought to show them your business plan. It'll encourage them to help you (because then you're not just a shmoe, you're a shmoe with a Plan), and they will often be able to make useful suggestions—along with destructive criticisms—about your plan.

BUSINESS BONES

Before working on the business plan, there are a few decisions you have to make. You've got to pick an appropriate name. You've got to pick the right legal structure. And you've got to comply with (or decide to ignore) some legal regulations.

The first thing you need is a name. Here are some guidelines to finding an effective one:

- **Don't be clever or cute.** Unless your target market is one of the very few that rewards cleverness, it's better to keep your ingenuity to yourself. Toy Cleaning Services is boring, but better than Tinkerbell's Tidy Toddlers. If your customers see a business card with the former name they know exactly what you do—and if they're interested in the service, they call, and you get paid.

- **Be descriptive.** Toy Cleaning Services is better than Diversified Children's Services or Smith Enterprises. (Never use "Enterprises"— it reeks of amateurism.) But, if you are thinking of expanding into a closely related area, you may want to have a name that can grow with you, such as Playground Cleaning Services, or Toy Cleaning and Repair.

- **Keep it short and simple.** Use Toy Cleaning Services, not Organization and Sterilization Services for Playthings and Playgrounds.

- **Think about using your own name.** Tom Travers Toy Cleaning Services. Using your own name has advantages and disadvantages. The advantage is that if you use your name in the business name, you don't have to file a DBA (a "doing business as" or fictitious business name statement). On the other hand, one of the most damaging things a business can do is be self-centered (by writing ads that talk about the business instead of the customer, for example), and giving a business your name instead of one that communicates with customers seems to epitomize entrepreneurial egocentricity.

The bottom line is, you need all the help you can get. If you can use your business name as a sales tool to describe the features and benefits of your business, do it.

Once you find the perfect name, check if it's already being used. Check the phone book and your city or county clerk's office. You can do more—check the trademark directories, write to your state's Secretary of State—but that's not necessary unless you're incorporating or want to go national.

Next you've got to decide the legal structure of your business. You'll almost certainly want to start a sole proprietorship. But if you're an optimist, in a committed relationship, or need some serious help, you might want to start a partnership. And because you may have always wanted to be an Inc., we'll mention corporations too.

- **Sole Proprietorship.** This is the easiest and cheapest business structure. One person owns and operates the business. In fact, the business is the person—you're taxed as an individual, are *personally* *liable* for business debts, and obtain loans based on your personal credit. We recommend starting as a sole proprietorship. You can always change later as your business grows.

- **General Partnership.** In a general partnership, you own your business with one or more partners, each of whom is involved in running the business. Make sure everyone knows exactly what's expected of them (and have it in writing), that general partnerships dissolve as often and acrimoniously as marriages, and that unless you have an agreement that says otherwise, each partner is liable for any and all business debts. If your partner skips town with $5,000 of your clients' money, you are legally responsible for the entire amount. Of course, the reverse is true, too, but we won't get into that. And taxes are much more complex for partnerships than sole proprietorships.

- **Limited Partnership.** A limited partnership has managing and limited partners. The managing partner(s) has full control and liability. The limited partner(s) has no day-to-day control of the business, and their personal liability is limited to the amount of their investment in the partnership. There are all sorts of tax ramifications for limited partners, so if you think this is the route for you, do some serious research or speak to a professional.

- **Corporations.** Unlike a sole proprietorship or partnership, the corporation is a separate legal entity. If you die, it lives on. The primary reason you'd want to incorporate is that in most cases, you have only limited liability for debts or lawsuits against your corporation. So if you're starting a high-risk business, like organizing rafting trips over Niagara Falls, talk to a lawyer about incorporation. Otherwise, deal with this once you can actually afford to hire that lawyer.

There are a few more legal annoyances. Zoning ordinances are an issue mostly for home-based businesses. There is zoning, for example, against on-site sales, deliveries, noise, signs, and employees. The responsible thing to do is talk to your Zoning or Planning Commission before you start your business, to see exactly what you can and can't do. The irresponsible thing to do is just go ahead with whatever you want until (and if) a neighbor or landlord complains about you. In that case, you may be fined. So don't say we didn't warn you.

Then you're faced with the Business License and DBA. For a business license, you generally have to fill out a form and part with some money at the city or county clerk's office. Our only advice here is that if the form asks how much you expect to make, write a low estimate. Otherwise, the government might develop a morbid interest in your taxes, which is never a good thing. If the powers-that-be discover you didn't get a business license, your punishment fits the crime: they make you get one. But to cover ourselves, we should mention that you *could* be fined.

Filing a DBA is different. If you'll be conducting business under a name other than your own, you must file a Doing Business As (or Fictitious Name Statement). Why? Because otherwise you can't deposit all those checks made out to your business name, that's why. And it's sort of fun. The first time we filed a DBA, we got this great rush of ownership—we had taken the leap and started our own business! (You can tell we don't get out much.)

One last thing: your Seller's Permit (or Resale Number). If you live in a state that has a sales tax, you're required to collect the tax and send it on to the state if you're reselling goods or providing a taxable service. And because only the final purchaser is required to pay sales tax, a permit allows you to buy goods for resale from a supplier without paying tax. Although we don't discourage some degree of fudging regarding zoning and licenses, do not use your resale number to buy tax-free stuff.

OK, enough with the legal notes. Back to the loving creation of your personal roadmap to sure-fire success: your business plan.

WE JUST LOVE IT WHEN A PLAN COMES TOGETHER

Your business plan will have six sections. In addition to describing your business—its purpose, benefits, and goals—you're going to do some math. In business, this is how you keep score: if the money coming in is greater than the money going out, you're winning. The way you plan to win is by setting the right price, making sales, and controlling cash flow. Don't worry, this all sounds worse than it is. If you're phobic about math, this won't be your favorite section of the book. But there's nothing like the feeling you get when your low estimate for sales and price and high estimate of your expenses combine to show a positive cash flow. Oooooh, we're getting goosebumps just thinking about it.

Your business plan will include your:

- business description (your goals, target market, resources, etc.),
- pricing,
- expenses,
- break-even point,
- other financial stuff, and
- marketing plan. But you won't be developing your marketing plan in this chapter—it is important enough to require a section of its own. After we show you how to create a super-effective marketing plan on a shoestring, we'll tell you to come back here to plug it in.

Business Description

We've included handy-dandy blank lines for your writing pleasure. You'll probably want to compile this information into a respectable-looking format at some point. But for right now, just jot down your thoughts:

Business profile: What products and/or services are you offering? Where? What makes your offer unique? What makes you the right person to start this business?

_____

_____

_____

_____

_____

_____

_____

_____

Target market: Who are your customers? You've already described them to some extent on page 116, but now's the time to describe them in detail. What were the results of your market research—what do they say they want, need, and can afford?

_____

_____

_____

_____

_____

Purpose/benefits: You've got to know what business you're in, and what your prospective customers want from you. There's an old saw about railroads failing because they thought they were in the train business instead of the transportation business. But if you're a dog groomer, you're not in the clipping business, you're in the dog health/beauty/love business. What benefits does your business confer to customers? Remember that a benefit is something the customer experiences, not something that describes the product or service.

_____

_____

_____

_____

_____

_____

Current situation: What trends and new developments will influence your business?

_____

_____

_____

_____

Competition/colleagues: Who else serves your market? They could be competing with you or offering complementary products/services. How do they market/promote/price their products and services?

_____

_____

_____

_____

_____

_____

Challenges: What are the main obstacles to your business success? How will you overcome them? Be honest. It's better to admit you don't know how to overcome an obstacle than to insist it doesn't exist.

_____

_____

_____

_____

_____

_____

Resources: Which of your resources can be used to help this business succeed? Describe them, how you'll approach them, and how they'll help.

_____

_____

_____

_____

_____

_____

Goals: Include your personal financial goals, setting them as high as you can without making them unattainable. And also describe your business goals. Do you want it to grow until you need to hire employees, or remain a one- or two-person business? Do you want it to be part-time or full-time? Is it the embryonic version of your dream business, or is it complete as is?

The last bit of goal-setting you should do is to write down specific, measurable goals that you intend to attain within a certain time: "I will sell at least forty cat breeder videotapes per month while spending no more than fifteen hours a week on the business by next October." Or, "I will contact twenty galleries every month starting in June." Many of your goals will be marketing goals, so return to this section when you finish your marketing plan.

_____

_____

_____

_____

_____

_____

_____

Pricing

Compete on any number of features: speed, guarantee, service, delivery, whatever. But don't compete on price alone. Someone will always underprice you, and, more importantly, you'll generate no customer loyalty—they'll switch to a cheaper competitor faster than you can say "Attention K-Mart shoppers." So cheap is bad. And know that *most beginning entrepreneurs underprice.* They're not quite sure if they'll get *any* customers, or if their products or services are all that good. Those may be legitimate concerns, but underpricing is never the solution.

Of course, you don't want to price too high, either. That's not to say that expensive isn't good—it is if you're providing an upscale product or service and have the image to match. And we've heard many stories about products that didn't sell until the price was raised, after which they flew off the shelves. Or consultants who unknowingly increased their fees tenfold due to a misplaced decimal point and got paid without a murmur. But in most cases the highest price you can get for your product or service won't return the most profit, because you'll sell fewer units.

Too cheap is bad. Too expensive is bad. So our advice is: *price just right.*

You're welcome. Well, actually, you've already researched pricing from the perspective of your customers and your competition. If you didn't do it then, check out your competitors' prices now. Call around pretending to be a client. Or if you're honest or something, call people in similar businesses outside of your geographical area and grill them. There are other methods of pricing, but asking people what they're willing to pay and researching competitors to discover what they're charging will work fine to get an initial price range.

Remember that if you'll be selling a product through retail stores, reps, or other sales venues that take a cut, the retail price of the product is probably more than twice the wholesale. When you're researching competitor's pricing, ask for the wholesale price. And when you're researching what your customers will pay for the product that you'll be selling retail, expect the retailers to take half of that amount.

Now you have a ballpark figure that seems to indicate what people are willing to pay. Reasonably enough, that's where you want to start. But start at the high end of the range—it's always easier to lower your prices than to raise them.

Your business plan should include your pricing, your rationale for your pricing (what research you based it on), and how you will test your pricing. You can't really decide on the optimal price until you test. Start with a high price. Offer a discount. Test a low price. Promote a super-high price for some special services. Try selling through discount stores or matchbooks. And each time you test, keep track of how much profit you made. Not how much money you brought in—focus on the amount of money you kept after paying all your expenses.

Be sure you don't sell your products or services for less than they cost you. This is not only possible, it's more common than you'd think. We know of a bargain shoe store that opened with fantastic prices. So good, in fact, that they were swamped. People were buying shoes hand over foot. The owners were thrilled, until they realized that they were losing a couple of cents on each sale. Every time someone bought a shoe, it was as if they'd just snatched a nickel out of the cash register. Those nickels added up and the shoe store folded like a broken lawnchair under a Sumo wrestler.

The moral of this story is: *you must know exactly what it costs for you to offer your product or service.*

Expenses

The first costs you have to consider are your personal expenses. Figure out your bottom line for one month of your life on the planet. Guess if you have to, but guess high—there will always be the occasional forgotten expense.

PERSONAL MONTHLY EXPENSES	$ AMOUNT
HOUSING	
Rent:	
Telephone:	
Utilities:	
SUSTENANCE	
Groceries:	
Restaurants:	
Daily coffee and bagel:	
Beer, wine, cigarettes, and all that:	
Therapy:	
DEBT	
Educational loans:	
Computer/car/stereo, etc. payments:	
Credit card payments:	
Friends bitching about the assorted amounts you owe them:	

PERSONAL MONTHLY EXPENSES	$ AMOUNT
FRILLS:	
Clothing:	
Gifts:	
Insurance:	
Transportation:	
Classes:	
Entertainment:	
STUFF WE FORGOT OR COULDN'T POSSIBLY KNOW ABOUT	
Stuff:	
Stuff:	
Stuff:	
More stuff:	
TOTAL MONTHLY PERSONAL EXPENSES:	$

Add it up. That's your monthly contribution to the national economy. That's somewhat pathetic. But it's also the minimum amount you need to pay for your life. That's terrific. The two of us can live, without altering our arugula lifestyle in any very substantial way, for about $1,900 a month. That's just $950 per author per month. If one of us were on a train going east at 44 m.p.h., and the other were…oh, forget it.

Anyway, we know we can live this cheaply because we've done it in the much-too-recent past. And it's really not all that bad. In fact, looked at from the right perspective, being able to live this cheaply is a great benefit. If you think about it, most startup business owners (that is, business owners who have all those traditional obligations) can't live for under $11,500 per year. So if you, like us, don't have three teenagers, a voracious mortgage, car payments, and the twisted desire to wear butt-ugly-but-expensive suits every day, you're ahead of the pack. Your minimum financial needs are probably all too obtainable.

The Cost of Doing Business

Other costs of your product or service include:

- **Startup costs.** These are one-time costs for anything you have to buy to start your business that you won't have to keep on buying on a regular basis. You'll divide your total startup costs by twelve to spread the expense out over a year—this way you can factor your monthly startup costs into your calculations.

START-UP COSTS	$ AMOUNT
Equipment:	
Supplies:	
Training/information:	
Licenses/fees:	
Other:	
More/other:	
TOTAL STARTUP COSTS:	$
TOTAL STARTUP COSTS/MONTH (Previous line divided by twelve):	$

- **Marketing expenses** (ads, brochures, postage, printing, telephone, commissions, give-aways, etc.). These are actually variable costs (which we'll discuss below), but when you first start a business, you won't be able to tell how much you have to spend on marketing to make one sale. You simply won't know how many sales will result from your ad or press release or networking or flyers. Once you've been in business for a while, you can determine marketing cost per sale. But when you're just starting out, use an estimated monthly marketing budget. Figure out how much you can afford to spend per month on marketing, then budget a little more than that.

TOTAL MONTHLY MARKETING BUDGET	$

- **Fixed business expenses.** These are expenses that stay the same regardless of how many products you sell or hours you work. Take rent, for example. If you sell one cat toy, you owe $300 a month for rent. If you sell 1,000 cat toys, you still owe $300. Your rent has no direct relationship to your sales volume—you have to pay it even if you don't sell one item, so it's a fixed expense. Remember to express annual costs for licenses, dues, and other expenses in terms of monthly amounts. Your monthly fixed costs are your business expenses for:

MONTHLY FIXED BUSINESS EXPENSES	$ AMOUNT
Rent:	
Most utilities (see variable costs, p.143, for the exceptions):	
Voice mail/mail box rental/ Internet connection:	
Licenses:	
Dues:	
Most office, store, shop supplies (see variable costs, p.143, for the exceptions):	
Insurance:	
Transportation:	
Legal and professional fees:	
TOTAL MONTHLY FIXED EXPENSES:	$

Then add up all the above to get your total fixed business and personal expenses per month:

MONTHLY EXPENSES	$ AMOUNT
Monthly personal expenses:	
Startup costs per month:	
Monthly marketing costs:	
Monthly fixed expenses:	
TOTAL MONTHLY FIXED EXPENSES:	$

This is what it costs for you to keep yourself and your business running if you never make a sale. You pay for food and utilities, you pay for startup office supplies, you pay for printing flyers and renting a voice-mail box, but you don't sell any products or hours. If you actually want to sell something, you've got to factor in the variable costs of making a sale.

- **Variable costs.** These include any expenses that lead directly to a sale or result directly from a sale. If it costs you twenty cents in catnip for each of your cat toys, and you sell ten cat toys in one month, your variable cost that month is $2. If you sell 1,000 cat toys, your variable cost for catnip is $200. Your costs per sale (not monthly) for variable expenses are:

VARIABLE BUSINESS COSTS PER SALE	$ AMOUNT
Cost of goods bought and sold (the wholesale cost of a product you sell):	
Cost of goods manufactured and sold (the cost of materials for a product that you make):	
Cost of goods repaired (the cost of repair supplies):	
Other cost of goods sold (any cost that is directly tied to a product you sell):	
Some office supplies (receipts, for example):	
Some utilities (if, for example, you spend $50 in electricity every time you use your kiln):	
Any other expense that's directly related to a sale:	
TOTAL VARIABLE COSTS PER SALE:	**$**

Knowing the total cost of making one sale is important. If the total variable cost to make one bronze candlestick is $10, and the average retail price of similar products is $11, you have a problem. But at least you know you have a problem. And don't think that variable costs are for products only. If you're starting a service business you have to figure the variable costs of any thing that goes along with your service (you give away a free mug or a do-it-yourself booklet, for example), of sales-related transportation, and of any other cost that is directly related to making a sale.

Remember: If you're starting modular businesses, the variable costs will be different for each business, but the fixed costs and your personal expenses will be divided up among them. Just because you'll be operating two businesses doesn't mean you've got to pay rent twice.

You'll probably be able to arrive at a fairly accurate estimate of most of your costs. But you can't accurately predict all of your costs. Your marketing budget is nothing more than a leap of faith, and your variable costs may be fairly sketchy, too. Well, welcome to the woolly world of business plans. If you don't know something, guess.

Before you guess, of course, you'll try to estimate the cost through research: talk to suppliers to determine the cost of materials and delivery, for example, or to competitors to approximate the costs of whatever they're willing to share with you. But if you can't figure it out, guess.

Fortunately, we have a powerful secret technique to help you arrive at estimations of unpredictable costs: guess high.

That's just about all you can do.

Break-even Point

Now you know how much money you need to take in before you can make a profit—your total monthly fixed costs. And you know what it costs for you to sell one product or hour—your total variable cost per sale. But exactly how many products or hours do you have to sell each month? How will you know when your income has covered your outgo? What is the minimum number of sales you have to make to stay afloat? The answer to all these questions is your break-even point.

Your break-even point tells you when your sales have covered all of your costs. Anything above break-even is profit. Anything below is pain.

You determine your break-even point by subtracting the variable cost per unit from the selling price to get the gross profit per unit. Then divide that number into the monthly fixed costs plus your personal expenses. Clear as mud. Here's an example:

Let's say you're offering harmonica lessons. First figure the variable cost per unit (and in this example one unit is one hour). Let's say you have to pay for copying music and giving away a free harmonica to every student. The copying will cost $.25 per hour. And the harmonica costs $17.50 which, when spread over the ten hours a student will probably work with you, is $1.75 per hour. So your variable cost is $2 per hour.

Now let's say that you've decided upon $15 per hour as a selling price (because that's what your research seems to indicate is fair to middling). Then subtract the $2 variable cost per hour to get $13 profit per hour.

Then divide your total monthly fixed costs by $13. Assume that you're starting two businesses at once. The fixed costs for the teaching business are $100, plus half of your personal expenses, which we'll say is $500 (the other business is responsible for paying the other half). So your total monthly fixed cost for this business is $600. You need to teach forty-seven hours of classes a month ($600 divided by $13 is about 47) to break even. If your students take one hour-long class a week, or four hours per month, you need to have twelve students per month to get those forty-seven hours.

Your break-even point is twelve units per week. If you sell fewer than that, you lose.

Maybe you think twelve regular students is realistic. But you also want to see what happens if you raise your price to $20/hour, which is the top of the range established by your market research.

The variable cost per unit is still $2. Subtract that from the selling price ($20), and you have an $18 gross profit per unit. Dividing your total monthly fixed costs (still $600) by gross profit per unit ($18) equals about thirty-four hours a month of classes to break even. That means you have to have nine clients per month, every month, paying $20 per hour, to break even. Depending on where you live, your resources, your marketing plan, your luck, and your cunning, that may be easy or it may be impossible.

	selling price	_____
−	variable cost/unit	_____
=	gross profit/unit	_____
	monthly fixed costs	_____
÷	gross profit/unit	_____
=	break-even point	_____

So now you know your break-even point. You know exactly how much you have to charge and how many sales you must make per month to keep the fridge stocked and the landlord quiet.

Your break-even point is when you begin to make a subsistence-level living—not a profit. You're still eating rice and beans six days a week and are totally unprepared for unexpected (yet inevitable) expenses. It's a good bottom-line figure to watch so you know you're not losing money, but unless you exceed your break-even point with great regularity, you'll be struggling to stay in business every month.

After you establish your break-even point, go back to the "Goals" section of your business plan. What are your reasonable financial goals? Plug those in where your personal expenses go, and run the break-even analysis again. Now that's what you're aiming for—a life of ease and plenty.

The Cost of Taxes

Taxes are yet another cost of doing business. But you won't know how big a cost until you've been in business for a while. Our rule-of-thumb is to figure that 25 percent of our income will go to taxes. If that's more or less true for you, can you still get by? If the government takes 25 percent, is it still possible for you to meet and exceed your break-even point? Or do you need to raise your prices, increase your sales, or lower your costs?

Total Cost Per Sale

Once you've been in business for a while, you should calculate your total cost per sale. This is similar to your variable cost per sale but more complete, as it includes all your expenses. The standard advice is that you should do a projected cost per sale analysis before you start, even though it will be meaningless because it's based on projected figures (read: guesses). Business books heavy enough to cripple a rogue elephant say you should do it. And if you love numbers and charts and graphs and such, go ahead. Otherwise, wait to calculate your cost per sale until you know how much you're actually spending on marketing, and how many sales you average per month.

Your cost per sale is simply the total cost of selling one unit (one product or one hour). First figure what your variable costs are per month by multiplying your variable cost per unit by the average number of units you sell per month. Then add your monthly fixed, marketing, and startup expenses to that number, but don't include your personal expenses. Divide the sum by the average number of units (products or hours) you sell per month to discover your cost per sale.

cost per unit _____
x   average number of units sold per month _____
=   variable costs per month _____

variable costs per month _____
+   monthly fixed costs _____
+   monthly startup costs _____
+   monthly marketing costs _____
=   total monthly costs (excluding personal expenses) _____

total monthly costs _____
÷   average number of units sold per month _____
=   cost per sale _____

That's what it costs for you to sell one unit, before your personal expenses and taxes. If you sell for less than that, you are giving money away. If you sell for precisely that amount, you are working for free. This is a good number to know, because occasionally you may want to work for free if you're running a promotion with a non-profit, for example, or offering a sample to an excellent prospect. But if you do it too often, it will drive you out of business and you won't have a cent for food or rent or other indulgences.

So add your personal expenses to your other expenses, and run your cost of sale again.

total monthly costs including personal costs _____
÷   average number of units sold per month _____
=   cost per sale _____

Now that's your true pre-tax cost of selling one unit. Staple that number onto your cerebral cortex and do not sell below it.

More Fun with Financials!

There are two additional financial reports you can include in your business plan. They are the sales forecast and the cash flow statement.

A sales forecast is when you say, "Well, maybe I'll sell fifty units a month. Yeah, that's right. Fifty a month." Then you run all the numbers to see what will happen if you sell fifty a month. But you also want to know what happens if you sell far fewer than you expect. Pick a depressingly low number. Do the math. Figure it out. Make sure you can live with it. Then market well enough to exceed it.

You also want to know what will happen if you sell far more than you expect. This may have actually happened a couple of times in the history of the world. But we love doing this calculation. "Hmmm. How much will we make if we get sixteen new clients every day? Millions! Haahaahaaa, we'll rule the world!" Pick a high sales estimate that's within the realm of the possible, and visualize, meditate, affirm, and bust your butt until you hit the magic number. Your high sales forecast can also be used to direct your marketing campaign, particularly after you've established your ability to meet or exceed your break-even point every month.

And then there's the cash flow projection. This is the most helpful document we've never made. It shows you, well, the flow of cash in and out of your business. It's a report that predicts projected income and expenses at the time at which you expect to actually receive or spend them. It usually covers a year, but is broken down by month, and shows you in advance if you will have no money to pay next month's bills, so that you can adjust your plans accordingly.

A cash flow projection will help you discover that, although you can sell $5,000 of goods next month, and only spend $1,000 to do it, you're in trouble. Why? Because you won't get the five grand for ninety days, but the $1,000 will be payable immediately. If you didn't run a cash flow projection, you'd spend your $1000 and then wouldn't be able to make the $5,000 because in the intervening three months your absolute lack of money would lead your landlord to evict you, your telephone to be shut off, and your fulfillment system to collapse.

Unfortunately, the cash flow statement works according to the law of HIHO—hooey in, hooey out. Before you know what you're doing, it'll be totally unreliable. And we think that, at the tiny end of the small business spectrum, a cash flow statement doesn't do much because you've always got just about zero cash on hand. It's not a crisis, it's a lifestyle. But if it sounds like you'll need it, the cash flow projection can make the difference between manageable growth and the most frustrating sort of failure.

Mastering Money-
Making Marketing

WE LOVE MARKETING. Not only is it fun and creative and challenging, but it's profitable.

Before you too fall in love with marketing, there are a few misconceptions to clear up.

- Marketing is not advertising. Advertising is one small part of marketing, and a part that many small businesses don't need to emphasize.

- Marketing is not sales ability. Selling can be a vital part of a marketing plan, or it can be mostly absent.

- Cash is not the most important need for marketing: creativity and persistence are.

Then what is marketing? Marketing is everything you do to promote your business. From the name you choose to the way you answer your phone to a publicity campaign, it's everything you do that will influence prospective customers' buying decisions. And all your marketing has exactly one goal: to create a customer. Not to be clever, funny, or innovative, just to create a customer.

Making a sale is never as important as creating a customer. The bottom line, of course, is selling. But the way to get there is by creating customers—loyal, satisfied, repeat customers.

Marketing is one of the major advantages you have in business. With a little ingenuity, persistence, intelligence, and this book, your marketing will be better than that of 90 percent of other businesses. We can say that with confidence because 90 percent of other businesses can't sell a life preserver to a drowning man.

That's because they don't know marketing. They think if they spend a small fortune putting a half-page ad in the newspaper every six months and go to networking groups where they talk about the weather and exchange enigmatic business cards, they've got a marketing campaign. That's an inane, expensive hobby, not a marketing campaign.

You, on the other hand, are going to create a powerhouse of a marketing plan. You're going to target a niche market and supercharge your business through word-of-mouth referrals and a unique selling proposition. You'll contact your prospects with a message that sells the benefits of your offer to the right people and motivates them to take action. And you'll do it all on your shoestring budget.

Oh, and we should mention the first, fundamental, golden rule of marketing: *have a good product or service.* If you're offering something shoddy, the better your marketing is, the faster you'll be out of business.

The Niche Market

We have mentioned the importance of targeting a niche market once or twice already. But in case you've forgotten, niche marketing is when you sell to a narrowly defined target market. You don't sell to "brides," you sell to Korean brides, or brides who are getting remarried, or Texan brides who play the accordion.

If you remember no other marketing tip, remember this: if you're marketing a product or service and you think that "everyone" has a need for it, you're doomed. When everyone in general wants something, no one in particular does. But if you're marketing a product or service that a very specific market niche needs, you're halfway home. You'll be avoiding direct competition from bigger fish and you'll be powerfully focused on providing tailor-made solutions to the needs of a very distinct group.

If you haven't decided on a target market, do so now. If you only have access to a limited market, your target will have to be less tightly focused than that of someone who can reach a larger market. You might choose "health" offices (meaning, say, medical, dental, chiropractic, and psychiatric) as your market instead of just one type of health office. Or you might have to choose upscale women instead of upscale single mothers.

Whatever. But know exactly who your prospective customers are, what they need, and how your offer benefits them.

As important as identifying a target market is identifying their needs or problems. *You're always selling solutions, not services or products—and you're selling them as benefits, not features.*

TARGET MARKET	PROBLEM/NEED	SOLUTION	FEATURES	BENEFITS
Serious hikers	Uncomfortable, poorly made hiking boots that cost a small fortune	Custom-fit, comfy boots with a three-year guarantee.	Triple sewn seams. Titanium eyeholes. Big fat sole.	Hike longer and more comfortably with a boot guaranteed not to fall apart.
People who own big dogs	The dogs don't have enough room to run around—not healthy for a big dog to be stuck in a small area.	A place for big dogs to run around and socialize.	Pick up dogs three times a week. Four acres of land to run on. Play with other dogs.	Keep your big dog healthy and happy with no hassle.
Aspiring writers	Writing is painful.	Self-hypnosis audiotape that helps writers enjoy and excel at writing.	Certified hypnotherapist. High-quality tape. Hypnosis works best for creative people such as writers.	Enjoy writing, write more, and write to the best of your ability.
Bar and nightclub owners	Need more people spending money on drinks.	Band that attracts hard-drinking, free-spending customers.	Play grunge/funk. Lead singer used to be in the Osmonds.	Fills the bar with paying customers.

You've got to know the needs and problems of your target market well enough to develop an appropriate, helpful solution, and translate it into specific benefits. And then deliver those benefits.

Let's say you're in the band mentioned above. Your benefit is "fills the bar with paying customers." That's a great benefit. But why should the bar owner believe you? Because you explain, "We have a 500-person mailing list. We'll send them all a notice about our gig and, if you give us a one-dollar-off coupon for a drink, we'll send it, too. After the first discounted drink, your bar will be full of customers paying full price. We'll also get people dancing and having fun by buying a drink for the best dancer several times a night. And we'll make sure our friend Bruno, the DJ at the college station, mentions that we're playing here. And we'll distribute 250 flyers around town the week before the gig. And..." You get the idea. If you were a bar owner, and two bands approached you, one with ideas about how to fill your bar with paying customers, the other with ideas about how wonderful their music is, whom would you hire?

If you're concerned about appealing to too few people because your market is so tightly focused, consider these two points:

- You'll make more money providing graphic design exclusively for alternative health practitioners than you would doing it for all small service businesses. You can identify their specific problems and needs and offer specific solutions. It's true that there are a hundred times more small service businesses than there are alternative health practitioners. But that doesn't matter: there is already such a surplus of designers serving "small businesses" in similar ways that none of them really stands out, whereas you can capture almost the entire population of health practitioners because you're the only one focused on their needs.

- And you can expand by offering depth, not breadth. What other services can you offer to alternative health practitioners? Marketing, record-keeping, event-planning.... Instead of being a designer who scratches the surface of many markets, you'll establish a mini-empire by serving one fully.

MIGHTY MOUTH

Generating word of mouth is a tremendously powerful marketing technique. Think about how it works in one of the most common situations. You go to Chez Pez, a new restaurant in town. The food's OK, but not great. And the waiters play hide-and-seek all evening. If you were in a good mood, you might forgive them. But you're not, so you get mad. You decide not to go back. Some of your friends want to go out to eat a couple nights later. "How about that new place, Chez Pez?" they say. "No way. The food's terrible and the service is worse," you reply. The next day one of your friends is talking to a co-worker at the Quick-E-Mart, and the co-worker asks if the friend has tried Chez Pez yet. "No way," sez the friend, "that restaurant is a short-cut to dysentery." The nine people in line at the Mart hear this, and they all go home and....

Well, you get the idea. Word of mouth is most efficient when it's negative. That's because poor service is rewarded tenfold, but good service is expected and not rewarded at all. We'll say that again: nobody talks about good service. So how can you profit from word-of-mouth marketing?

Because that rarest of all beasts, spectacular service, is rewarded very well. People are often unaware of this, because they never give or receive spectacular service, and because it's so much easier to complain than recommend. In fact, every time one of your customers gets poor service, the chances are that she tells between ten and twenty people about her negative experience. So before you let anyone walk away dissatisfied, imagine that it's not just one person, it's a mob of angry ex-customers. Then abase yourself (we'll get to that in a moment). Also accept the fact that for every ten customers willing to complain about terrible service, there are only one or two who'll praise fantastic service.

But you can up those odds. Giving spectacular service sounds like a cliché—what business aims for mediocrity? But there are five specific things you can do to give spectacular service and encourage the resulting word of mouth:

Exceed Expectations

This is the big one. Don't promise more than you can deliver. In fact, promise less. Surprise your customers with some extra value. Lee brought some clothes to a local dry cleaner. One of the shirts had a small tear. When she picked up the clean clothes, the tear had been mended. They did it for free, and didn't even mention that they'd done it. Now, we have no idea if they're better dry cleaners than the competition. But we used them again because of that little repair job. They mended another little tear for free. Now we won't go anywhere else and we recommend them to friends. They've transformed us into walking advertisements—and all it cost them was two minutes with a sewing machine. That's good business.

Think of a way to give your customers more than they're used to getting. Offer a little extra something of value and related to your business that brightens your customer's day and keeps you on the tip of her tongue. The more a customer spends on you, the greater the value of the gift you offer. And it doesn't have to be something that costs you money—an extra hour of service, a free evaluation, or an add-on service will do fine.

Avoid Annoyances

Have you ever seen one of those signs that suicidal small businesses post: "A Lack of Planning on Your Part Does Not Constitute an Emergency on My Part"? Annoying. Or a business that solicits your money through the mail but won't ship the product until your check clears? Annoying. They're saying that you should trust them, a faceless company, to send you a quality product before they'll trust you to send a valid check. How about a business without an answering machine? That doesn't take returns? That doesn't offer a guarantee?

Remove every hassle you can. Sometimes this is tough. You'll have trouble getting a merchant account for accepting credit cards, for example. If there's an unavoidable hassle, acknowledge it, apologize, and offer something to make up for it. This is another cliché, but the customers really are the most important part of your business. Serving a customer cannot take you away from the truly important part of your business, because serving customers is the most important thing you do.

Defuse Dissatisfaction

Sometimes customers will hate you. They'll think your product or service stinks, your haircut is offensive, you're charging too much, you're offering too little, whatever. We have some pearls of wisdom for you from Jerry Wilson's *Word-of-Mouth Marketing,* which is a very good book on generating positive word-of-mouth to get new customers, launch new products or services, and control disasters. When you've got an angry customer, do five things:

1. Acknowledge he's upset. You might feel stupid, but say, "I can see you're angry." This won't fix anything, but it's a whole lot

better than "Well, dogloaf, if you weren't such a complete loss, this never would have happened," or even, "Oh, sorry, you must have misunderstood me."

2. Make a sad/glad statement. "I'm sorry my doghouse collapsed on your poodle, and I'm glad you told me about it."

3. Make an action statement. "I will fix the problem."

4. Ask the magic question. "What will make you happy?" Then, if it's possible, do it. It will almost always be perfectly reasonable, and you will have transformed a customer who would have spread a horror story about you to one who has to admit that you did the right thing.

5. Do something extra and unexpected. "And, in addition to the new doghouse, I'd like to pay to get Fifi groomed, as a way of making up for the trauma."

If the customer is absolutely, unquestionably, completely wrong, still do the above. You have an excellent chance to convert an angry customer into a satisfied, repeat customer who will spread the good word about you. When you come across a truly evil customer, who you know will give you no end of grief, still make him happy. And if you don't want to, you never have to do business with him again.

Reward and Request Referrals

We've heard of a housepainter who, having completed his financials like a good boy, figured that his profit per job was about $4,000. His problem was that he wasn't getting much work. There were enough painters doing quality work that none of them could really take off without a major marketing blitz. So the painter devised a blitz: he offered $1,000 in cash to any of his clients who would refer him to a new client who ended up using his services. Now don't think that we encourage a one-dimensional marketing campaign—nothing could be further from the truth—but that was all he needed to do. He never had to look for work again.

That's a great story, but you're probably not going to be making four grand of profit per job. Sure, if you're making a $40 profit you can offer a referral fee of $10, but it's hardly the same. You want to offer something with a high perceived value and a relatively low cost, relative to the new business your client brings in, that is. It might be a month's free housecleaning, once a referred client has worked with you for over a month. Or a free pair of cowboy boots when a referred customer buys one of your hand-tooled saddles. Remember to run the numbers before you start a full-on referral reward program, though. You don't want to reward yourself out of business.

The very minimum you should do to get referrals is ask. There are many ways to do this. Some are pretty hard-core: sitting down with a client and saying, "Who are five (or however many) people you know who would be helped by my services?" That's a far more effective way of getting referrals than asking, "Do you know anyone who'd be helped by my services?" You set a goal and expect them to reach it. Still, most people will say, "Gee, I can't think of anyone right now, but if I do, I'll give you a call." And you never get those referrals. So you come back with, "Well, who are your five biggest suppliers (or favorite clients, or best-dressed friends, or most athletic acquaintances, or...)?" If you're a pushy type, and your client is enthusiastic enough about your services to warrant that approach, the two minutes you spend asking for referrals could be the most valuable you spend.

If you're uncomfortable putting clients on the spot like that, don't do it. Instead, focus on spectacular service and a "soft-sell" request for referrals. But even if you're wimpy about it, you must ask for referrals.

Solicit Suggestions

That head really should read "Welcome Complaints," but we wanted to stay alliterative. Make sure your customers know you welcome complaints. Give them every opportunity to complain. Why? Because if they have something to complain about they'll either say nothing, and never do business with you again, or they'll complain, you'll fix the problem, and you'll continue doing business together. The vast majority of customers who are willing to spend the time to tell you what's wrong with your business have some interest in maintaining their relationship with you. This is tremendously effective market research. And if one person complains, that means that ten others feel the same but weren't willing to mention it—so do what's necessary to fix the situation.

You can include a "Please Complain" form with products you're shipping, with follow-up mailings you send after completing a job, in take-one boxes, whatever. Get the word out that you want to hear the worst. Then fix it.

WARNING: Word-of-mouth marketing, though potent, is almost never sufficient. You've also got to be pulling in new clients with other marketing techniques. When you hear a business owner say, "Oh, we don't need to do marketing, we get all our business through word of mouth," that really means one of the following: they're not doing any business; they're doing great, and in the not-too-distant future they will be desperate for customers and will have no idea what happened; they're lying; they're doing marketing but don't know it; or they're tremendously lucky. None of these is a solid basis for a marketing campaign.

THE MOST IMPORTANT CUSTOMER IN THE WHOLE WIDE WORLD IS...

...not the richest, nor the most gullible. No, it's the customer who's already purchased from you. All too many businesses that have effective marketing strategies focus on attracting new customers to the exclusion of serving and selling to previous customers. This is bad, bad, bad, bad. If possible, attracting repeat customers should be the backbone of your marketing effort.

Yes, we know you can't have repeat customers until you actually get customers in the first place—we will be getting to that soon. But once you've sold something to someone, focus on offering them more complete, frequent, newer, or additional services or products. They already know what a good job you do—they've bought from you and have been satisfied, and you have a relationship. They are the perfect prospects for any related offer. Never take them for granted.

MAKING AN OFFER THEY CAN'T REFUSE

The first step toward developing an irresistible offer is to identify your Unique Selling Proposition. This is the reason that prospects would buy from you instead of a copycat competitor. It's the benefit you offer that none of the other businesses selling a similar product or service offer. Sometimes this is self-evident, like if you're the only business on earth that specializes in tattooing octogenarians. Otherwise, work to make your unique selling proposition explicit:

- Pizza in thirty minutes or less.

- Financial aid consulting that's free if it can't save you over $500.

- Hand-crafted furniture in any color you choose.

- The dating coach who guarantees you'll be dating within two months if you follow the advice.

- Marketing consultant who only charges a percentage of money brought in.

The most common unique selling propositions are based on price (lower, higher, offering credit, barter, etc.), availability (overnight delivery, extended hours, recurring offer such as a blank-of-the-month club, etc.), selection (size, quantity, color, etc.), service (delivery, free offer, guarantee, personalization, etc.), or location.

Every business needs a unique selling proposition. The ones mentioned above are fine. You've got to do at least that much. But they're not great. They're not so attractive that you wish we'd included the phone number of the business because you want to call them right now. To create that sort of urgency, you have to transform your unique selling proposition into an irresistible offer. The goal is to make prospective customers think, "I'd have to be an idiot not to say yes to this."

Build on your unique selling proposition by offering something for nothing (or for very little) and a very strong guarantee.

Say you're offering hand-crafted furniture in any color. That's nice, but it's not going to light up the switchboard. But if you offer a free two-month in-home trial period—you do the custom coloring and deliver the furniture for two months, after which your customer can just ring you up and have you retrieve the stuff without any obligation— then anyone who's looking for expensive, hand-crafted, perfectly matching furniture would have to be an idiot not to give you a chance.

But what about the risk? What if all your furniture gets returned? Good questions. There are four answers.

1. One of your jobs as a successful entrepreneur is to take the risk instead of imposing it on your customers. So stop kvetching about risk.

2. All you're really doing is offering credit with no payments for the first two months and a money-back guarantee. Neither of those things is so revolutionary. It's just the way you are expressing them that's unique.

3. Your furniture is good, and people are lazy, so once it's installed, very few people will return it.

4. The extra volume of furniture you sell due to your irresistible offer will more than make up for whatever returns you get (and can then re-condition and sell anyway).

Then offer an incredibly strong guarantee, because the last thing you want is dissatisfied customers. Make sure you phrase your guarantee emphatically: "If you are not 100 percent satisfied that my services exceed your expectations, for any reason at all, I will refund every penny with no questions asked."

And if you've got the nerve, you can even do something like this: "If you are not completely satisfied, I will refund 150 percent of the money you spent. That's right. If you're not satisfied, I'll give you money just to apologize for the inconvenience." Or instead of offering extra money back, offer an additional product or service with a high perceived value.

We wouldn't have the courage to use a guarantee like that in a mail order offer, where people can ask for a refund without actually meeting you. But with a service business, or any business where the customer has some contact with you, the vast majority of customers will not ask for their money back, even if they are not completely satisfied. Of course, the vast majority of your customers will be satisfied. But even those who aren't usually won't ask for a refund. So the risk isn't nearly what it seems.

Before you make an irresistible offer, though, ensure that the offer is legitimate. There can be no fine print, as this utterly defeats the purpose. And the person to whom you're making the offer must be part of your target market. Don't offer a free rose garden as a premium for landscaping to renters who move every four months.

Sometimes the irresistible offer is, well, resistible. In these cases, all you can do is just do the best you can. You don't want to go so crazy, though, that you make everybody happy but yourself. But it's pretty tough to offer too much to someone who is truly a member of your target market.

LEVINSON'S LAWS

The last thing to mention before we start discussing the actual marketing techniques is Levinson's Laws. Jay Conrad Levinson wrote a book called *Guerrilla Marketing.* It's the bible of the marketing-on-a-shoestring books. Being anything but an idiot, Jay kept writing and created a "Guerrilla Marketing" empire. The following are our top picks from his most important marketing secrets:

Be Committed

Make a marketing plan. Think about it. Revise it. Brainstorm. Revise it again. Then implement it and commit to it. Do not abandon your marketing program prematurely! Think of marketing as an investment. If you stop marketing before you get results, you lose your previous investment.

Be Consistent

Smaller, more frequent contact is better than larger, less frequent contact. It's far better to have a small classified ad running every week for a year than a full-page ad once a year. And once you decide upon a media, a message, or a style, stick with it. Only after you, your friends, your mother, and your dog are totally tired of it will your prospects even begin to notice it. Keep it consistent.

Use an Assortment of Marketing Techniques

Diversity is a wonderful thing. Incorporate it into every aspect of your marketing program. The best way to do this is to go through the next chapters and choose all the techniques that can build your business. You may have to drop a few while making your marketing plan, but you still want a well-rounded, diverse group to attack your marketing target from all sides.

Make Profits After the Sale

We've already talked about the power of repeat customers. Here's how Levinson says it: "Marketing doesn't end with a sale; instead, it's the marketing you do subsequent to the sale that leads to the juicy profits. It costs five times as much to sell to a new customer as it does to sell the same thing to an existing customer."

Use Measurement

Businesses that have mediocre marketing, which is most businesses, don't know it. If they measured how much money they received for every dollar they spent on ads, for example, they'd be horrified. And rightly so. You have to ask people where they heard about you, track how much you make from customers attracted by your assorted marketing techniques, and know exactly how well each one pays off.

Fine. You're ready to consistently commit, measure, profit, and diversify. But what exactly do you do to attract loads of cash? You read the next chapter.

Your Marketing Tool Kit: A Directory of Low-Cost, High-Profit Marketing Techniques

THE BEST LOW-COST MARKETING techniques in the world are yours for the taking—just browse through this chapter. Whenever you find one that seems appropriate to your business or your personality, write it down or dog-ear the page or highlight it. Choose as many techniques as you can. You'll be discarding some of them later, and the more you end up with, the more money you'll make.

COPYWRITING

We're starting out of alphabetical order because copywriting is the foundation of many marketing techniques. And the tips you learn in this section should be applied to non-written marketing techniques as well.

As far as copywriting—and being 100 percent sales-centered—goes, the guy you need to listen to is Jeffrey Lant. He writes incredibly forceful books that give us a headache after about 100 pages. They're also the best books we've seen on writing marketing materials that *sell*. Lant mentions twenty-one copy commandments. We prefer ten, though, because we're traditionalists. (If you're looking for a comprehensive discussion of copywriting, investigate one of Lant's books that we mention in the Resources section at the end of this book.) If you humbly follow these commandments, your marketing material will be the best around.

The Copywriting Commandments:

I. Be Selfless. Self-centered copy is the bane of all marketing. You know you're being self-centered when your business name is on the top of all your marketing documents, you talk about your business history, your business philosophy, your products or services, your wonderful abilities. *But your prospects don't care about you.* They care about themselves. Focus your copy on them: their problems, needs, solutions, actions. And focus it on one individual prospect—write to "you" not to "clients."

II. **Be Beneficial.** Don't talk features when all that prospects want are benefits. Never say "Tom's Toy Cleaning Services uses only the latest sanitation equipment, has a flexible schedule, and bills monthly." No one is buying sanitation or schedule—those are features. What they're buying are benefits—healthy kids, attractive play areas, easy recordkeeping, no scheduling hassle. Lead with benefits, follow with features. This is important—focus on customer benefits, not product or service features.

III. **Be Simple.** The world of marketing is overflowing with clever, artistic, innovative ads that grip your imagination but don't sell a damn thing. You don't have the luxury of spending piles of cash without selling anything. Your marketing materials must *sell*. Keep them simple and focused. Stress benefit after benefit, sell the solution, and make it imperative to respond immediately.

IV. **Be Repetitive.** Focus on one major client-centered message that you hammer home again and again: Redundancy is your pal. You know your prospects' problem, you have a solution—appeal to their self-interest time and again until they feel the urgent need to respond.

V. **Be Immediate.** Give your prospects a reason for acting *now*! If prospects don't respond to your offer immediately, the chances are that they won't ever respond. Make them an irresistible offer (expressed as a cash value, if possible) and combine it with a benefit and a time limit. "The $50 Aura Cleansing Kit is yours absolutely *free* if you respond by May 2."

VI. **Be Explicit.** You must tell your prospects exactly what to do next and what will happen when they do it. "Call 555-5555 and leave your name and address." Or: "Drop this postcard in the mail and I'll call you to schedule a free evaluation."

VII. Be Generous. Give your prospect a reason to buy more now. This is one of the reasons you should always try to develop a "line." If you can offer more solutions to your prospects' problems, do so. Offer a package deal, up-sell to a more complete service or product, or provide the same benefit in a number of ways.

VIII. Be Empathetic. You understand the anxieties of your prospects, so demonstrate that connecting with you is the only sensible thing to do. Show that you understand your prospects' problems and that doing business with you is risk-free. Provide precise information about what, when, how, and where your offer will benefit the prospect. And, of course, be reputable and guarantee quality.

IX. Be Praised. Use testimonials. And not just any testimonials— testimonials by people just like your prospects who are willing to have their full names used and who will focus on the benefits of your offering. (More on testimonials can be found below.)

X. Be Guaranteed. Guarantee satisfaction. You already read about guarantees in the section on developing an irresistible offer. Well, do it. Guarantee satisfaction and be satisfying.

One more thing about copy. Although there's some disagreement about this, most expert copywriters recommend writing long copy instead of short copy and lots of white space. Fill your ad, letter, brochure, or whatever with words: benefits, offers, incentives, more benefits, features, guarantees, testimonials, explanations, and even more benefits. Don't be concerned with white space. You've already targeted prospects who have some interest in your offer. They want information, so give it to them.

ADVERTISING

Advertising is in the beginning of the directory only because it's alphabetically correct, not because advertising is the primary marketing technique. We'll say it again: advertising is *not* the most important marketing technique. But done correctly, when your ad is totally focused on getting a response, it can be a powerful addition to your marketing plan.

To get the most out of your advertising, make sure that:

- you're *committed* to running your ad many times,

- the publication *targets* the right market,

- your *offer* is compelling,

- you sell *benefits* instead of features,

- you motivate and make it easy for your prospects to *act now* (whether it's calling for more information, cutting out a coupon, or getting a special deal), and

- you remove the risk with your iron-clad *guarantee.*

You probably already know where you want to run your ad—you're selling to a familiar target market and you know what they read as well as what they need. But you've got to know if the publication is worthwhile as a sales tool. One way to check is to look for ads selling similar things. If they've run in every issue for a year, they're making money. That's a good sign. But you can't be sure if they're making money on the up-front offer (what you see in the ad) or on the back-end offer (what they sell once they get you on their mailing list). So it's a good idea to buy what they're selling and see what else ends up in your mailbox. Then duplicate their success by structuring your similar, but far superior, offer in the same way.

If you're running an ad to sell a product or service, you probably don't want to use the one-step method: trying to sell the product or service in the ad itself. This may work with excellent full-page ads or with low-priced (under $10 to $15) offers, but usually you're better off with the two-step method: asking your prospect to respond for more information, a free sample, a discount, or whatever. Then you follow up with sales letters. Repeatedly contact the people who respond. Send a series of at least three follow-up mailings.

Once you run an ad, you *must* test it. You have to track the number of responses you get and the number of sales that result. Then subtract the cost of the ad (and the subsequent letters, etc.) from the profit you made. If you lost money, and you've given the ad a fair chance, something's wrong. Make a better offer, ensure that you're stressing benefits, check that you're targeting the right market, and so on.

If you're running several ads, you've got to know how many responses are due to each ad. If the prospects will be phoning you, ask where they saw the ad. If they'll be writing, "key" your address. Use "Make Balloon Animals, Suite 4D, 111 Main Street, Fresno" in one ad and "Make Balloon Animals, Suite 3C, 111 Main Street, Fresno" in another. Or key with your business name—"Balloon Animals, 111 Main …," "M.B.A., 111 Main…," and "Balloon Animal Fun, 111 Main…." Or anything else. Just be sure you know exactly how much you're making or losing due to each ad.

If you want to find all of the places where your ad might work, go to the library. Check out Standard Rate and Data's *Business Publishing Advertising Source* and *Consumer Publication Advertising Source*, Bacon's directories, *Burrelle's Media Directory*, and any of the other directories in the same section. You'll be surprised at what you can find—at the very least you can check out ad rates, circulation, and editorial profiles to see if the publication matches your target market. You also might dig up a publication you didn't know about. Give them a ring and ask for their rate card and a sample issue so you can see if it'd be appropriate for your ad. And once you know a publication's circulation and ad rates, you can figure out how much you're paying per subscriber, and can compare the costs of advertising in different publications.

ANSWERING MACHINE MESSAGE

"Hi. I'm not in right now. Please leave your name and number, and I'll be sure to get back to you as soon as I can." That, and all the varieties of it, is the worst possible thing you can do on your answering machine. Someone's called you because they're interested in your offer. Don't give them the cold shoulder—sell the benefits of working with you instead. "Hi. I'm out organizing a garage sale that will bring in the maximum possible amount of profit. If you'd like my free tip sheet listing the ten biggest mistakes people make when having a garage sale, leave your name and address. Or just leave me a message, and I'll get back to you as soon as I can."

ATTITUDE

Be nice. It's goofy, but it's a powerful marketing technique. You don't really think about it until you run into a small-time entrepreneur who breathes fire and stinks of sulfur—and then you buy elsewhere. When you feel the urge to do evil, see your customer as a $10 bill instead of a person. You wouldn't rip up that bill no matter how mad you were. Don't rip up the person, either. And remember to be nice on the phone and fax and e-mail, too.

Be quick. The only thing that makes up for slow service is tremendously nice service. And even that pales if you have to wait long enough. People often value their time more highly than their money, and for good reason. If you don't waste the first you'll get more of the second.

Be enthusiastic. This business is paying for your life. Be enthusiastic about it.

Smile—it works. It's so rare to be greeted by a happy, smilin' business owner that people take note. And they return. (Also, people can *hear* when you're smiling. So smile when you answer the phone. Really. Try it.)

Always think like your customer. What do you do that would piss you off if you were that customer? Stop doing it.

Be clear. If there's anything in the least confusing about your business (and there always is), make sure you patiently explain and guide people through it as if they are morons. We wanted to brew our own beer for our wedding and went to a micro-brew shop to ask how to do it. The guy there was nice enough, but he was talking a different language. All we wanted was for the guy to take us by the hand and say, "Buy this. Buy that. Combine them like this. Do that. Wait a while. Then you'll have beer." Instead, he confused us until we stumbled out in a daze, our wallets unopened.

AUDIO- AND VIDEOTAPES

If you're selling something to a list of very hot prospects, think of using audiotaped or videotaped sales pitches. They're more memorable, informative, and persuasive than written material alone. And few people will throw them out (if they're attractively packaged) without giving them at least a moment of attention. Or produce an informational audio or video that also contains a sales pitch. For example, a dating coach might give away a cassette called "The Six Secrets of Body Language," which includes helpful tips and the benefits of using the coach's services.

BARTER

Bartering offers two benefits to your marketing campaign. It saves money, which you can then spend on other marketing techniques. And it attracts customers who are themselves creative marketers and can easily be converted into your personal fan club. Look on all barter partners as great potential word of mouth. You've already worked out a win-win situation—now build on the momentum. Refer customers to each other, share ideas, and work out a cross-promotion plan (see below).You can either create your own bartering opportunities, which takes some digging, or work through a local barter network.

BROCHURES

Most startup businesses feel obliged to spend money on a brochure. They think having a brochure proves they're really in business. But unless the brochure is packed with client-oriented benefits and an incentive to act immediately to get those benefits, it's not worth much. If you're selling to several markets, have brochures for each, explaining how you meet their unique needs. And don't be afraid to fill up the brochure with copy: testimonials, benefits, solutions, your offer, more benefits, and more testimonials.

BUSINESS CARDS

Business cards are a vital part of your marketing campaign, except when they're not. If you don't use them, don't buy them. And if they don't sell your business, there's no reason to use them. But they can be tremendously effective mini-ads for your business. Guess which one of the following will bring in the cash:

Window Washing Service

Wanda Squeegee
President
(555) 555-5555
122 E. Grubb Avenue
City, State Zip

Improve Your Image
Get Clean Windows!

Call before _____ for a FREE window washing!!!

Call Wanda Squeegee at (555) 555-5555
Window Washing Service

Other things you can include on a business card are a map or directions to your place of business, a coupon, a price list, testimonials, useful information that will turn your business card into a reference tool, or a customized offer.

CANVASSING

Knock on doors. All you need is knuckles, a business card, a smile, appropriate clothing, and to read the section on selling (below). This is a low-cost, highly effective method for selling *if* you correctly target the people you're canvassing. If you're selling expensive hand-crafted mailboxes and you target wealthy homes with fine everything but boring mailboxes, you might be on to something. If you're canvassing an apartment building, you might not.

CREDIT

In a business where you must offer credit, you must offer credit. But offer some serious incentive to pay up front—a valuable free evaluation, an extra hour of work for every ten hours paid for in advance, a free widget holder. You want to get that money in your pocket without dealing with collection, for collection is the bane of good clean fun.

On the other hand, offering credit may be your unique selling proposition if you do it for a product or service that doesn't usually offer credit. That's OK. But figure that about 5 percent of the people who buy on credit won't pay. Factor in some money for sending them a series of friendly little reminders and a friendly little phone call. (Just because they're deadbeat scum doesn't mean that you want them spreading negative word of mouth about you).

Cross-Promotion

This is one of the most powerful and overlooked low-cost marketing possibilities. For a complete discussion of cross-promotion, read Jeff Slutsky's book *StreetSmart Marketing*. Although he focuses on retail businesses, the ideas are transferable, and effective.

Let's say you're offering ice sculpting services. Here's the three-step method of starting a cross-promotion:

1. Find noncompetitive businesses that have the same customers as you, or employees who fit your customer profile. Since your ice sculpting customers are people having events such as weddings, noncompetitive businesses include event planners, party rentals, florists, wedding consultants, caterers, and so on.

2. Approach them with a coupon for your business—$50 off an ice sculpture. Tell them that you'll put "Compliments of [their name]" on the coupon, and they can give it as a premium to their customers or prospective customers. It's a nice little gesture. What does it cost them? Nothing. You print it up, and they just hand them out.

3. Print up a professional-looking coupon with the offer and the "compliments of" section. Give them to your promotion partner and listen to your phone ring.

Slutsky says there are three benefits to running a cross-promotion: cost, control, and credibility. The cost for distribution of the coupons, usually a major factor, is zero. You control the people who get it by giving it only to appropriate partners. And—perhaps the biggest benefit—your credibility is very high because you're working with established businesses.

Cross-Promotion Variations

Give away other businesses' coupons as a premium. If you know owners of appropriate businesses, however slightly, explain the benefits of a cross-promotion to them and give away their coupons.

Or organize a two-way cross-promotion, in which the baby clothing shop gives away your coupon for a handmade rattle with every purchase of a playhouse, and you give away their coupon for 15 percent off any baby shoes.

COMMUNITY INVOLVEMENT/CHARITIES

Of course you might want to sponsor a Little League team or put an ad in the local symphony program. But unless you're reaching your target market by selling symphonic appreciation classes or something, those are donations, pure and simple. They're not marketing.

If you want to market through community involvement or charities, you can use a modified cross-promotion. You know all those nonprofits that sell raffle tickets, chocolate bars, and magazine subscriptions? Let them use your gift certificate or "donation dollar" as a giveaway. In addition to asking people to buy a chocolate bar for $1, the buyer could get a $5 gift certificate to your business. Your only expense is printing. The distribution is free and you're helping a worthy cause raise more money.

If there's a particular local cause you want to help, you can give them a day's or week's profits (depending on what sort of business you have). Then they'll market your business for you. You won't make any money on the day or days of the event, but you'll jump-start your repeat business, develop a loyal clientele and a mailing list, get loads of free press, and make a lot of friends.

There are opportunities for businesses and nonprofit organizations to help each other, and as a savvy small businessperson, it's your job to find them.

CONTESTS AND SWEEPSTAKES

The difference between a contest and a sweepstakes is that a contest requires that the winner use a skill to win, while a sweepstakes is entirely a game of chance. There are laws regulating both of them, so if you're going to be getting big-time publicity, make sure you're not violating any of them.

A well-done contest requires prospect participation, stirs up excitement and awareness of your business, expands your mailing list, and leads directly to sales. A poorly run contest is more hassle than it's worth and alienates all those prospects who don't win. Our recommendations for running a profitable contest sound just like our recommendations for everything else: make sure you've targeted the right market, use the contest to explain the benefits of your business, and develop a situation in which everyone wins.

COUPONS

We like coupons. They offer a quick-and-easy benefit to users, and motivate them to spend money *now*. They're sort of the "no-brainer" of marketing: if you don't want to develop something truly creative and engaging (or are having marketer's block), a coupon will always do. A little creativity—an unusual offer, distribution channel, "look," or any other novelty—always helps, of course, but if you hit your target market with a coupon for something people want, you'll probably do OK. And if you're going to go through the trouble of developing, printing, and distributing coupons, don't let them fail due to a weak offer. When was the last time you bought something because it was just 10 percent off?

The downside is that it's possible to use coupons as a crutch and destroy any price credibility you once had. This isn't a problem when you're just starting up, of course. But if you find yourself relying heavily on coupons, try to ascribe responsibility for your coupons to someone else—compliments of a non-profit, for a special occasion (such as Ramadan or New Year's), or as a premium to valuable customers.

Make sure you offer coupons for a limited time only. This encourages prospects to act immediately, although, of course, you'll probably want to honor any expired coupons as a customer service. And mention the benefits of doing business with you on the coupon itself.

CUSTOMER APPRECIATION

If some of these marketing techniques are repetitive it's not just because we're lazy bums. It's because they're important and we want to graft them onto your cerebrum, and the best marketing is repetitive. You do the same thing over and over again. You keep doing it. Redundantly. Repetitiously. Continuously. Customer appreciation is one of those things. Never let a customer get away without expressing your appreciation in some way—with a smile, a thank-you, a thank-you note, a follow-up phone call, whatever. If you consistently, genuinely, and noticeably show appreciation for your customers, most of the other marketing techniques are just gravy, because you've perfected the basics.

DEMONSTRATIONS/CONSULTATIONS

You know your product is great. Now show your prospects. You can either demonstrate your product or service at a store, fair, conference, show, or office, go to people's homes to show how it would work there, or let them take it home for a trial period. Stress the benefits and, if possible, have your prospects actually use the product or service. Nothing sells better than a good experience. It's why car salespeople are always trying to get you to take a test drive, and it works.

If you're offering a free consultation, keep it between forty-five minutes and an hour, and either close the sale at the end of the consultation, or follow up soon thereafter. Be at your best: offer value, not just a sales pitch; stress customer benefits; and be efficient, easy to work with, and wonderful in every way.

DIRECT MAIL

Although almost every category in this chapter is the subject of several books, only a few of them are the subjects of an entire genre. Of those, direct response is the most written-about. If you're going to make it a foundational part of your marketing plan, a short discussion here can't cover everything you need to know—look in the resources section for recommendations. But direct response can also play a more limited role as one of the most focused, powerful, and cost-effective weapons in your marketing arsenal. There are very few businesses that wouldn't benefit greatly by the use of a well-conceived and well-executed direct response campaign.

The List

The first and most important ingredient in a direct response campaign is your mailing list. You can have a brilliant service, a wonderful offer, and a fantastic sales letter. But if you're selling lace doilies to *Soldier of Fortune* subscribers, you're not about to get rich quick.

Here are the six best ways to get a mailing list:

1. Offer to send a free brochure, special report, catalog, newsletter, premium, or other incentive to anyone who contacts you. If people respond to an appropriate offer, they are your target market. Put their names and addresses on your list.

2. Ask. Ask your satisfied customers, networking contacts, and cross-promotion partners if they know the names and addresses of people who could use your offer. Then give them an incentive for helping you out. And ask for names yourself through a guest book, a warrantee card, etc.

3. Run a contest, such as one of those business-cards-in-a-jar promotions, where customers put their card in a fishbowl and the one that is picked gets a prize.

4. Swap for them. You can exchange your mailing list or your products or services for someone else's list.

5. Assemble them. Look in the phone book, and check the library for directories. Dig up all the addresses you can find and make your own list.

6. Buy them. Look under "mailing lists" in your phone book, call up the list companies, and ask for their catalogs. There are an amazing number of lists out there. They can be expensive and may require high minimum orders, but if they truly target your market they're probably worth it.

The Letter

Copywriters get thousands of dollars to write direct mail letters, because they're the second most important part of the mailing. If you haven't got thousands to spend, you'll have to do some research and write your own sales letter. Here are a few hints to get you started:

■ Develop a powerful, benefit- or problem-oriented headline or first sentence. (Use a headline if it's clear that what you're sending isn't personalized. Otherwise, use the first sentence.) You've got to pull the prospect into your letter immediately.

■ Use a personalized salutation (and correct name) if you can.

- Use your letterhead to present a benefit. Have a tag line under your business name that says "Helping Your Dog Live in Perfect Health" or whatever.

- Use bullet lists and indented paragraphs to make the letter easy to read and to highlight benefits.

- Separate your risk-free guarantee from the rest of the copy in a framed box or on a separate piece of paper.

- Use testimonials.

- Present a "call to action" that tells the readers exactly what to do and what will happen when they do it.

- Give a reason (a discount, early-bird special, premium, etc.) for ordering immediately.

- Offer premiums as an added benefit for ordering *now*.

- Explain what awful thing happens if the reader doesn't take action.

- Always use a P.S.—it's the second most-widely-read part of a letter. Use it to call for immediate action, present an incentive, reiterate the iron-clad guarantee, or reemphasize the primary benefit.

- Use a gimmick. Attach a dollar bill (it costs money, but it's guaranteed to get attention), a handwritten Post-it note, a packet of Sea Monkeys, or anything else that will make it harder for the recipient to ignore your letter.

The Envelope

If your mass mailing looks nothing like a personal letter, put a "teaser" on the envelope. That's a short phrase like "Look inside for a way to extend your dog's life by up to five years!" that gets people to open the envelope when it's clearly junk mail.

Our recommendation, however, is to make your letter look like personal correspondence:

- Don't use an envelope teaser.

- Don't use a self-mailer.

- Don't use labels. Either hand-address it or laser print directly on the envelope.

- Use a first-class stamp.

- Use only your name and address for a return address—no business name.

The Response Device

Make it easy for prospects to contact you, and ask them to do so repeatedly. If you make it easier to respond (with a postage-paid envelope or a toll-free number, for example) you'll get many more responses.

If you're using a reply envelope, you need an order form. Because people often throw away all the information but the order form, you should make this a self-contained and complete marketing device. It should have the benefits, unique offer, guarantee, and call to action printed on it. And don't call it an order form: it's an acceptance certificate or upgrade card or risk-free trial request application.

Direct Mail Postcards

Postcards are less expensive than letters, don't get thrown out without being opened, and have a tremendously high readership rate. Use postcards to keep the solution that you're offering foremost in your prospects' minds, complete with benefits, guarantee, and testimonials. Make the postcard a coupon, offer a free report to people who call the phone number and leave their name and address, etc. Although it's tough to close a sale with postcards, they're great for qualifying leads and starting a two-step sale. Use them if you can.

The Card Deck

Card decks are collections of 50 or 200 postcards or index cards packaged and mailed together. You share the costs of postage with the other card-buyers, so you can have a card mailed to tens of thousands of prospects for just pennies per card. There are card decks targeting many markets. Check the Standard Rate and Data and other business reference books in your library to see what's available, or talk to a mailing list broker you find in the phone book. Card decks can be a great way to generate leads.

Inserts

Find a direct mailer who's already targeting your group. The best way to do this is to browse through the magazines your group reads and request info from all the ads that would be attractive to your target market. See what you receive. If it's a professional-looking offer that's not directly competitive with your offer, you might be able to work together. You'll print up inserts selling your services or products and, for a small fee per piece, the direct mailer will include them in her mailing. The benefit to you? Low-cost promotion to a targeted market of very hot prospects. The benefit to your insert partner? Because you pay some fee per piece, decreased costs lead to increased profits.

Testing

Because there are so many variables involved in any direct mail campaign, you won't know which of the techniques you used are responsible for your brilliant success or abject failure without testing. If direct mail will be an important part of your marketing mix, develop several different mail packages and track the results from each one to see which does best.

Catalogs

Your ultimate goal may be to produce your own big glossy catalog, offering everything you can to, say, large dog owners (that is, owners of large dogs, not large owners of dogs), or tea drinkers, or whatever. That's fine as an ultimate goal. But first you need to start slowly, with a small line of products. Build a mailing list and a group of satisfied customers. Do some publicity. Work out the bugs in your fulfillment services. Expand your line. Promote yourself. Eventually, you'll have a catalog. Don't start with twenty-five products and wing it. Start small and build organically.

You can also sell your product through an established catalog. Find a catalog that sells products that appeal to the same target market as your products. Then call them and ask how they review new products. Be warned, though, that catalogs require a very high mark-up. If your retail price is only three or four times your cost, most catalogs won't be interested.

DIRECTORIES

The Mother of All Directories is, of course, the phone book. For a small business, a Yellow Pages ad is usually unnecessary. If you're starting an offbeat, difficult-to-categorize business, it's almost certainly unnecessary.

On the other hand, if you're starting a business that fits perfectly into a Yellow Pages category—landscaping, for example—you probably ought to buy an advertisement, after you generate enough profits through alternative, low-cost marketing techniques to know that the ad isn't your most crucial marketing resource. Then test the results of your Yellow Pages ad to see if it's worth it, or if you can better spend the money on incentives, cross-promotions, and publicity events. Also, if you do run an ad in the Yellow Pages, never direct customers to it because they'll find your competitors as well. Instead, direct them to your White Pages ad, where you're all alone. There may be other directories you could list in, perhaps for free. Check out *Directories in Print* to find appropriate directories.

DISPLAYS AND SIGNS

In retail, 70 percent of buying decisions are made at the point of sale. This is why Point-of-Purchase (POP) displays and signs are so important. So don't be shy—have your POP display or sign tell consumers all about the benefits of your product. We know that you're probably not going to start a retail store. But if you're selling through retail, think of offering a free display to any retailer who buys a minimum amount of your goods. (Look under "Displays" in the phone book to find a custom display manufacturer.) Or you can offer posters or shelf talkers, those little signs that hang from the shelf your product is on. And make sure the POP display or sign is as good as your best ad.

DOOR HANGERS

If you're offering a product or service like meal delivery to a local target market, you might want to try door hangers. They're not laser-like in their focus, but they're cheap and effective. Don't go too cheap, though, because this is already a sort of down-market technique. Use quality paper and a color or two for a professional impression.

EDUCATIONAL PROGRAMS/PUBLIC SPEAKING

Offer workshops, seminars, classes, or speeches. With a product-based business you can teach how to make it, how to fix it, how to use it, how to buy it. With a service-based business you can teach how to do it yourself, how to get the most benefit from it, how to avoid the ten worst mistakes in it, how to hire a consultant to do it, and so on. This is a very powerful technique if you are a dynamic speaker and can offer the attendees a good value. If you're not comfortable with public speaking, it would be worth your while to attend a public speaking class just so you can take advantage of this technique.

We suggest offering the educational program for free and then profiting in four ways:

1. Publicity. A free program is an event. Write up press releases before and after the program (see the publicity section, below).

2. Credibility. When you're a teacher or speaker, you get immediate, priceless credibility if you meet or exceed the expectations of the audience.

3. Build Your Mailing List. Ask all the attendees to write their names and addresses in a guest book, and soon you've got a list of hot prospects who are interested in what you're selling and have seen what a hot tamale you are. Then follow up with a thank-you-for-attending letter that happens to contain an irresistible offer as well.

4. Sales. Never use your soapbox to deliver a sales pitch. People came for information, not sales, so deliver everything they expect and then a little more. At the end of your class or speech mention that you're making a very special offer (your $199 weight-loss package for only $99) to thank people for attending.

EVENTS

Hosting an event is a great way to generate publicity, build your mailing list, network, make sales, and profit in oodles of other ways. The only problem is that it's not easy. Actually, you need some serious organizational skills to pull it off. But if you've got what it takes, think about hosting a conference, seminar series, fund-raising event, awareness-raising event, goofy publicity event, contest, celebration, festival, or jubilee. Make sure you get media attention and, if it's successful, think about making it a regular occasion.

FLYERS AND CIRCULARS

If your target market lives, parks, passes, or shops in a certain area, you can use flyers and circulars to attract immediate attention to your offer for just pennies. You can put them under windshields, stack them up in offices and stores (with permission, of course), post them on bulletin boards, or hand them out on the street. With good copy and the appropriate market, you can convert this cheap marketing technique into fast cash.

FOLLOW-UP

This is what separates the savvy entrepreneur from the corporate cog. There are two kinds of follow-up, both of which are absolutely vital to making your business as successful as it should be:

1. If prospects exhibit serious interest in your offer (that is, they know what you're offering and go out of their way to respond to you), follow up. Send a series of letters and postcards keeping in touch and making offers, explaining benefits, and providing solutions. Make phone calls. Get them that information they asked about.

2. And when they finally buy from you, it's time to get serious about follow-up. They've just joined the elite group of your most important customers. Send a premium, a card, a newsletter, or an exclusive customers-only offer. Make sure they are satisfied with your product or service. Ask for feedback and complaints. Ask what else you can do for them. Offer new, improved, and additional solutions. Keep in touch—satisfied, repeat customers are the only job security you have (or need!).

FREQUENT BUYER PLANS

Encourage and reward customer loyalty with a frequent buyer plan. You can offer your own services—every sixth reflexology session is free, for example. Or you can offer a related service, and combine a frequent buyer plan with a cross-promotion: every customer who has six reflex-ology sessions gets a free herb garden design plan. And everyone who hires the herb gardener for two months gets a free reflexology session. If you're a networker by character, you can set up incentive programs with other small businesses and offer your customers a smorgasbord of possibilities, while offering a premium that costs you nothing and con-verting incentive-seekers into paying customers.

GIFT CERTIFICATES

Offer them. If your product or service is too strange to be given as a gift, definitely offer them and then use the offering as the basis of a pub-licity campaign during the gift-giving holidays. And if your product or service is a perfect match for gift certificates, what are you waiting for?

GIFTS: ADVERTISING SPECIALTIES AND PREMIUMS

Everyone loves getting presents. And giving them is a time-tested marketing technique. What a happy coincidence.

The difference between ad specialties and premiums is mostly tim-ing. You give ad specialties to prospective customers to encourage them to buy. You give premiums to people who have already bought from you to encourage them to buy again and spread the good word.

Ad specialties can be nothing more than a waste of money. When was the last time you decided to patronize a business based on its key-chain or calendar? Probably never. And, unless you incorporate an offer into your ad specialty or it's a perfect match for your target market, no one else will either.

How do you incorporate an offer? If you're giving away a calendar, include the coupon of the month. If you're giving away a mug, offer a free cup of coffee to anyone who comes to your booth with the mug. A perfect match would be a refrigerator magnet for a weight-loss consul-tant or an exotic fish in a little goldfish bowl for an aquarium service.

Premiums are easier. They can be more valuable, because you are pay-ing for them out of profits and they're directed at your most precious commodity: the customers who already know how wonderful you are.

You can offer a premium as a bribe for a testimonial, a referral, a complaint, or anything else you want from your customer. Or you can build a mailing list by offering premiums to customers who phone or mail in their addresses. Be creative. People appreciate appropriate gifts and respond to them. What does your business need? Can you get it by giving stuff away?

GUARANTEES

Guarantees are terrific. A longer-term guarantee is better than a short one. If someone has thirty days to decide if they ought to pay $90 for your newsletter, they may lose their nerve on day twenty-eight. If they have 120 days, your newsletter will be a part of their life before they have to make the final decision, and they'd feel guilty about getting their money back after such a long time, anyway.

We know a hypnotherapist who offers "Satisfaction Absolutely Guaranteed or Your Money Cheerfully Refunded." Well, other hypnotherapists don't know how he does it. There's some percentage of people who don't respond to hypnosis, so doesn't he lose his shirt on them? Here's his secret: He gets twice as many clients because of his guarantee, 90 percent of them are entirely satisfied, and only a tiny fraction of the remaining 10 percent ask for their money back. Plus he can charge higher rates because there's no risk to the client. So offer the strongest guarantee you can without losing sleep—and then live up to your promises.

INTERNET

The Internet changes rapidly, so be prepared to research the latest trends. In fact, how-to-make-money-on-the-Internet books are popping up faster than blemishes on prom night. We're not going to discuss how to get online, what a modem is, how to pick an ISP, or how to find newsgroups. If you're not familiar with any of that, focus first on other marketing tools. You can always pick up the knowledge later. Here we'll suppose you know the basics of the Internet, and just need an overview of how it can be used for marketing.

E-mail, Newsgroups, and Mailing Lists

The Internet is a fantastic tool for networking, and e-mail is becoming (or has become) essential for most businesses. So if you don't even have an Internet account, get one for the e-mail alone. If you don't have a computer, try getting an account at one of the many Internet service bureaus, such as Internet cafes, that are riding the wave of the hype. While writing this book, we e-mailed some of our favorite small business authors, and never failed to get a response. By the way, our e-mail address is GenerateE@AOL.com. Feel free to e-mail us with complaints, questions, haiku, or any sort of feedback.

Networking online is much the same as conducting market research online, which we discussed earlier. If you play an active role in an appropriate newsgroup or mailing list, you'll probably make some valuable contacts. On the other hand, the Internet, being a medium in which the masses can interact without the oppressive presence of the media or other elite, is chock-full o' jackasses and morons. That's not to say that the best and brightest aren't spending time online as well. But they're significantly outnumbered.

Let's say you are a computer consultant specializing in the VxWorks real-time operating system. You probably want to be involved in the comp.os.vxworks newsgroup. Maybe your target market consists of sexual abuse survivors. You might want to check out alt.sexual.abuse.recovery. If you can find an appropriate newsgroup or mailing list, join the discussion as actively as you can. Be polite to everyone. Offer valuable information and advice. And make sure your signature file presents the benefits of your business very clearly, and includes your e-mail address and the addresses of your Web page and autoresponder.

An autoresponder is an e-mail address that automatically responds to any incoming e-mail with a previously prepared sales letter, information sheet, or brochure. If you have one, prospects don't have to feel awkward about approaching you directly—they can just get your electronic brochure and see if your services meet their needs. And many autoresponder services can capture the names of people who e-mail. Send prospects a brief personal e-mail several days after they inquire to give them more information or make a special offer.

The World Wide Web

The World Wide Web, that most highly hyped of all Internet technologies, is not the marketing panacea we've all been waiting for. Instead it's a slow, embryonic technology. Right now marketing on the

Web is usually no more effective than a good doorhanger campaign or frequent-buyer program. So treat it as just one of your many marketing techniques.

But a good Web page can bring in business. You have to do more than develop a page, register it with the various search engines, and count your money, though. You have to actively push your Web page both online and offline. Include your URL in your sig file. Get links from other complementary pages. Mention your URL in every bit of marketing material you have. Then make the site interesting. Offer valuable information (such as can be found in one of your tip sheets or special reports), a contest, a free sample, or a special offer. And don't forget to change the content of the site regularly.

Do not load your Web page with lots of four-color art. That makes it slooooow. Use text to present your benefits, offer, guarantees, and testimonials. Use graphics very sparingly to highlight important elements, not as the basic lure of the page.

Advertising and Informing

The big online services have areas that are used for classified and banner advertising. Some charge for it, some don't. And there are several very large newsgroups that cover items for sale. Post your ads in all of these places. Then re-post your ads, since information on the Net has a shelf-life shorter than buttermilk in August. You can also participate in an "online mall." These electronic malls are collections of businesses that offer their products or services in the same place. If in your research you often come across the same online mall, and it's related to your business, you might want to look into renting advertising space there.

Another way to advertise online is to write an information sheet (see Special Reports, below) that offers useful information. Upload it to the online services libraries, ftp sites, and a gopher server, and make it available through your Web page.

Spamming and Bulk E-mail

We're assuming that you are familiar enough with the Internet to understand the blind rage that surrounds any discussion of spamming and the practice of sending unsolicited or "junk" e-mail. Luckily, we don't have such a personal investment in the Internet that we particularly care about netiquette. But we do think that, as of this writing, spamming has lost its efficacy as a marketing tool. When it first started, people actually read and responded to spam. Sure, most of them hated it, but it's true that the early spammers also made impressive amounts of money almost overnight. No longer. The spammers have spammed the spamness out of spam. It just doesn't work well enough anymore to be worth the mail-bombs and flames.

Bulk e-mail may not have reached that point yet. With bulk e-mail, you use software to strip the e-mail addresses from newsgroups and other message areas, such as the ones on AOL and CompuServe, that are related to your offer. Then you e-mail all of the addresses with your offer. Or you can work with a company that does the stripping for you, and maintains a list of tens or hundreds of thousands of e-mail addresses. We expect that at some point the profusion of bulk e-mail will negate its usefulness. And the good citizens of the Net are already finding ways to avoid receiving bulk e-mail. But as of right now, some people are getting small-but-profitable responses to their bulk e-mailing. If this appeals to you and you want to learn more, post a message on an entrepreneurial or network marketing newsgroup—you'll be buried in bulk e-mail before you know it.

There are other, more complex opportunities for selling online, such as starting your own newsgroup. If marketing online will be the foundation of your marketing effort, you ought to know about these methods. Otherwise, it's safe to ignore them.

Don't get us wrong—we do believe that the Internet offers many opportunities for businesses. You can send updated information to prospects, conduct online surveys, announce new products or services, create an online newsletter, offer technical support, do market research, or find a mentor. And it's even a valuable addition to your marketing plan. But in most cases, it'll only be an addition, not the central feature.

LETTERHEAD

Incorporate one of the benefits of your business into your letterhead. Don't just give your business name and address—include a tag line: "Window Displays Guaranteed to Increase Your Bottom Line," or "Helping Graphic Designers Double Their Income."

LOCATION

Unless you've got plenty of extra cash and much related experience, we discourage starting a retail business. But if you're going to start one anyway, realize that the cliché is mostly true. The three most important factors in the success of a retail store are location, location, and location. Clever marketing can compensate for many drawbacks, but if your type of store traditionally relies on walk-by traffic, a mediocre location will probably be your downfall.

MENTORS AND ADVISORS

If there are experts in your field whom you really respect, try to get to know them. Take their classes or seminars, ask to see their studio or office, offer them pertinent information or assistance. If they like you and see some promise in your business, ask them to be your mentor or advisor. Having an established expert take an interest in your success is a tremendous advantage.

If you have an extensive network, you can get several experts (one for production, say, and one for marketing, and one for design) involved in your business. If they're well-known, ask if they'd be willing to be a part of your advisory board, and put their names on your letterhead.

NETWORKING

Some people can't help but network. We have a friend who can't browse in a bookstore for fifteen minutes without learning the names, aspirations, fears, and phone numbers of four strangers. As you can imagine, we don't shop for books together anymore. But we do envy her ability to engage absolutely anyone in small talk—it's a powerful, time-tested, and all-around great marketing technique that costs nothing but time and can result in fame, fortune, friends, and fun.

If you can find groups or clubs targeting the appropriate market, you're halfway home. Also take classes, volunteer for community organizations, participate in events, and talk to the bartender. Don't worry if there are no groups, clubs, or associations for your target market— every opportunity to chat is an opportunity to network.

The bottom line of successful networking is this: Know what you want to get, and what you have to give, and then ask nicely and give generously.

You might want to *get* a recommendation for a good printer, feedback on how well ads in the local paper perform, and advice on how to keep your tomato plants alive. And you might also want to get leads, prospects, clients, and sales. But there's no better way to stop a conversation than to say, "I'm desperately seeking clients." Instead, what you want to get is someone who fits or knows about your customer profile: "Do you know if there's a kayaking club in town?" Don't be shy about your agenda, and don't keep it hidden. Be honest and ask.

You might be able to *give* advice on buying computer hardware, a recommendation to an interesting Web site, your impression of living in Japan, or information about new products for kayakers. Don't limit your giving to business—offer whatever help you can. Many networkers focus on getting what they want. And that's fine. But the best way to get what you want is to help other people get what they want. Listen to their needs, assist as well as you can, and people will go out of their way to reciprocate.

One last thing—although giving out your business card is a good thing to do, it's not a networking strategy. If you're not connecting to people through actions (theirs or yours), you're not networking.

NEWSLETTERS

Producing a well-done newsletter can be a tremendously profitable use of your time. You can offer your newsletter as an incentive to prospects: "If you order NOW, you'll get a free subscription to *Healthy Dogs* newsletter—a $99 value." And you can offer it as a gift to customers, the most valuable people in your business world, to encourage repeat business, remind them how wonderful you are, and invite referrals.

Make sure your newsletter:

- Presents solutions to the readers' problems. The most common mistake found in newsletters is that they offer entirely self-centered "news" about the company, and not useful information for the readers.

- Is short. Four pages is great. You can use a single double-sided 11-by-17-inch sheet of paper, fold it in half and then into thirds, and make it a self-mailer.

- Is readable. Keep the words, sentences, and paragraphs short. Use bullet and number lists, underlines, and graphics to emphasize important points and break up long chunks of text.

- Is regular. Monthly or bimonthly is best. Quarterly works, but not as well. You want to make it impossible for prospects and customers to forget your problem-solving abilities.

- Is fun. Why not? Your goal is to make recipients look forward to finding your newsletters in their mailboxes.

And don't be shy. Include an exclusive special monthly offer to newsletter subscribers only, testimonials, and a reminder of your guarantee and the benefits you offer. You're trying to do more than keep in touch and spread the good word—you're trying to make a sale.

If the response to your marketing newsletter is strong, think about converting it into a profit center as an information-for-sale newsletter. It's already targeted to your customers, and could add some lucrative depth to your "line."

PARTIES

You've heard of Tupperware parties. You've probably mocked and derided them. But if you have a suitable product and a friendly market, home parties could be a very effective way to sell yourself. You can start by organizing parties yourself, and then encourage your clients to have parties themselves. What's in it for them? A percentage of the take, or a higher percentage of credit toward buying your goods. If you have a small, tightly-knit market and some fanatical customers, it is possible to make big money with small parties.

PUBLICITY AND SELF-PROMOTION

Publicity is huge. It's responsible for a couple truckloads of how-to books, so we can't include anything like a complete description of it here. (See the resources section for our favorite books on publicity.) But we can tell you that it is a MUST. It's powerful and cheap. This is a marketing technique you want to learn and use regularly. Exploit the media—that's what they're there for. The benefits of publicity are:

- Low costs. Paper, postage, and time is all it takes.

- High credibility. People expect *you* to say you're offering an excellent product or service. But when the media, whether it's a newsletter, magazine, or radio station, say it, people believe it.

- Expert reputation. If you are quoted often enough, you become an expert. You get quoted more often. Buyers, who like to work with experts, come to you.

- Low sales resistance. People usually read sales literature with a grain of salt. But with publicity they can pore over all the benefits of doing business with you without much obligatory skepticism.

- Tremendous response. If you target the right media with publicity that focuses on solutions to problems that readers face, and make it easy to contact you, you may be surprised by an avalanche of inquiries.

The primary tool of a publicity campaign is the press release. This is a one- or two-page news story about the problem your business addresses and how to solve it—and, as it happens, how to contact you for a more complete solution. Here are the elements of a successful press release campaign:

1. Target appropriate media. Consider whatever your niche market reads, including local, trade, or niche media such as newsletters.

2. Target specific editors. Call the publication and ask who should receive a press release about your topic. Make sure you spell that person's name right.

3. Develop a "newsworthy" angle for your headline. The media will not print anything that seems sales-oriented, self-serving, or hyped. But they will print something that is targeted to the readers, addressing their concerns and offering valuable information. So, "Rod Glossop opens business selling pre-packaged herb garden kits" is too self-centered to be news. And "Buy Glossop Gardens' herb garden kit and start a flourishing herb garden for just pennies a day" is too sales-oriented. But "Too busy to grow the herb garden of your dreams? Here are seven easy tips that will save you time and lead to a beautiful, bountiful herb garden" is more like it.

4. Customize your "angle" for different publications. The headline above might be fine for *Executive Gardener* but "Discover the healing power of home-grown herbs" might be better for *Gardening for Health*.

5. Present the facts: who, what, when, where, and how? Not about you and your business, though—about the problem your raise in your headline. So "who" doesn't refer to Glossop Gardens, but to busy gardeners. And don't forget to write the facts in terms of problems and solutions (benefits). Use quotes—they're interesting, break up blocks of solid copy, and can provide credibility and a testimonial-like presentation of the problem. And don't be shy about quoting yourself.

6. Include contact information. You're not writing just to help the publication fill some pages—you want the readers to be able to benefit from your product or services immediately. They can't do that unless you include contact information. Try something like: "Rod Glossop is the owner of Glossop Gardens, which sells kits guaranteed to result in a low-maintenance, high-yield herb garden. To receive a copy of his booklet "Using Your Herb Garden to Achieve Optimal Health," send $1 to...or call him at (555) 555-5555."

Some people recommend following up a press release with a phone call. Some don't. Unless you have information to add, such as a tie-in with a news story, we don't think it's worth it—the last thing editors want to do is spend time on the phone with you lying about having received your press release. If they don't run it, send another one. And another. And another.

You can also write articles or columns as part of your publicity campaign. Many of the smaller, more tightly targeted publications are often looking for well-written, informative copy. And instead of going for the big bucks (that is, payment of any sort), either get an advertisement in exchange, or include a hard-selling final paragraph that presents the benefits of your business.

Or just write a book. Sure, it's a bit longer than an article. But you wouldn't believe the kind of people who are writing books these days. And being a published author provides a lustrous patina of credibility.

Once you get publicity of any type, milk it for all it's worth. If you get a good review or a positive write-up, make a zillion copies and include it in everything you send out. One of the problems with publicity is that it's so short-lived. But if you reprint like crazy, it can last years. Have a copy framed and placed in a prominent spot where you work. Use it as a testimonial. Use it to justify more media coverage. You get the idea.

Oh, and one last thing. After you get media coverage, write a thank-you note to the reporter or editor. And then keep in touch. The media is a hungry beast, so feed it.

REFRESHMENTS

This one's pretty simple. If you get together with prospects for any reason, feed them. Food is love.

SELLING

There are approximately 1,284 books about selling currently available. And that doesn't include the audio- and videotape courses, the seminars, newsletters, magazines, lapel pins, bumper stickers, and daily meditation calendars. In other words, it's a big subject. Luckily, we have a strong preference for one particular approach, and are more than willing to share it with you.

The problem with selling is that it's manipulative, painful, degrading, terrifying, and otherwise ugly. That's because you're usually trying to convince people to do something they don't want to do. Most of the selling books teach you how to do this well—they teach "closing" strategies to help you close the deal, how to overcome objections, and how to ask for the order over and over again, until the prospect finally cracks under the pressure.

Pretty hard-core ways to make a sale. And we've been suggesting some fairly hard-core marketing techniques. We think that hard-core is the way to go in your written marketing material. Hard-sell customer-centered benefits and incentives are great on a piece of paper. The prospect has an easy time saying "no" to a piece of paper.

But when you're selling in person, it's a different story. If you manipulate a prospect into buying, you lose in the long term. *Making a sale is never as important as creating a customer.* A prospect who feels manipulated will not buy from you again. If you're always working to overcome objections, you set up an adversarial relationship with your prospect, which doesn't help your chances of making a sale, and is tremendously frustrating and fatiguing. And if you approach the buyer from a position of powerlessness—basically cringing and begging to get the order—you're going to burn out quickly.

Enter the hero: High Probability Selling. HPS is a sales paradigm that does three things: it saves time, it reduces anguish, and it makes sales. It also contradicts much of conventional sales wisdom, but, because it's based on some fairly common-sensical notions like "don't waste time on prospects who don't want to buy," the untrained salesperson (that's you) will probably wonder what the fuss is all about. Take our word for it. Despite its glaringly obvious merits, High Probability Selling is revolutionary. And it's the best selling method we've encountered.

It was developed by Jacques Werth, who very kindly responded to our e-mail plea for some information on HPS oriented toward you, the shoestring entrepreneur. He wrote that the three most important concepts of HPS are:

1. Disqualify your prospects. Instead of convincing people to buy, you want to disqualify all but the High Probability Prospects, those prospects who need your product or service and want to buy it now. Your job is to find those prospects, not to try to convince other prospects (who don't want it) to buy. Focusing on disqualifying the low probability prospects instead of converting them makes the whole sales process much less painful and much more effective.

   Many salespeople hear this and are afraid. They think they can't disqualify any prospects and still make money. But trying to "sell" a low probability prospect takes a tremendous amount of time and effort and is very often unsuccessful, especially in the long term. Focusing on those people who want what you're selling is more efficient, respectful (of them *and* yourself), and profitable. This means that, when a prospect isn't interested, that's not a rejection—it's exactly what you want to know. You don't try to change her mind, you just move on to the next prospect.

It also means that you will end most sales calls before the prospect does. If you're not talking to a High Probability Prospect, you just say goodbye. And if you haven't done traditional sales, you don't know how liberating that is.

2. Do not try to convince prospects to buy. Recognize that High Probability Prospects resist being "sold." They want to buy from someone they trust and respect—not only does it feel better personally, but it indicates they've bought something that doesn't require a dog-and-pony show to be sold, something that can stand on its own merits. In fact, researchers have found that people will forgo lower price and better features to deal with someone they trust and respect. They trust you if you're offering a beneficial product or service without manipulation. If you tell them what you have, ask what they want, and see if you can do business together without artificiality and a honeyed tongue.

3. Disqualify prospects who won't make firm commitments to do business. This is hard. You've got a prospect who expressed interest in your offer. But you still can't ram your offer down her throat, no, you've got to get a commitment before proceeding. You do this by asking what the prospect's conditions of satisfaction are—exactly what price range, time limit, services, colors, features, etc. she wants—and then asking what the prospect will do if you can meet all of the conditions. If she doesn't say that she'll buy from you if you meet all of her conditions, end the conversation. If you can't meet the conditions, tell her so, offer an alternative, and ask if she's willing to proceed or if your inability to meet the condition means you should end the conversation.

As an example, suppose your prospect says, "I need someone to come in and do my window displays, but I can't afford more than $200 a month. And they'd need to be done on Tuesday before 8 A.M., and I'd want to have them changed at least three times a month."

You can't meet all those conditions, so you say, "For $200 a month, I can change the windows twice. Or for $300 a month, I can do them three times. Is one of those alternatives acceptable to you or not?" That last sentence takes a lot of nerve. It feels as if you're asking the prospect to tell you to take a hike. There are three reasons you say this anyway. First, you need $100 per display to pay the rent. Second, even if she does tell you to take a hike, you'll be getting hired by the manager of the next store before a traditional salesperson would be done trying to make the first sale. By quickly and easily weeding out the stores that are not High Probability Prospects, you have that much more time to find *good* clients. Third, if she truly wants what you're selling, she'll agree to have her windows done just twice a month, she'll respect you for not trying to manipulate her, and she'll know (or think) that she's dealing with a professional, not some funny-looking kid she wouldn't hire to sweep the floor.

Let's assume she says, "I guess it's OK to just have a new display twice a month."

You ask, "Are you sure?" She says she is. Then you ask for a commitment: "So if we agree on how to do your window displays twice a month for $200, before 8 A.M. on Tuesdays, what will you do?"

"I'll hire you."

Notice that you don't ask for the order. In High Probability Selling, you *never ask for the order*. Instead, you make mutual agreements and commitments. If you can meet the conditions of satisfaction, your prospect will work with you—and you let the prospect ask you to do the work.

There's a whole lot more to High Probability Selling than we can cover here. We very highly recommend Werth's book *High Probability Selling* to anyone who'll be selling on a regular basis.

SHOWS

Although some businesses avoid trade, craft, and other shows entirely, there are many businesses that get virtually all their clients though trade shows. If there's a trade show that's targeted to your market, you can supercharge your sales and—even better—develop relationships with the hottest prospects. Don't assume this means you need to rent a booth. You might just attend a trade show, and network like fourteen caffeine-addicted LAN administrators. Or, if you must present your products and make the immediate sale, rent a booth and remember to:

- Pick the right show. Ask around. Talk to people in the field. Get some expert advice. Find a mid-sized, appropriate show. Don't do the huge national shows until you have all the wrinkles ironed out (volume pricing, delivery, fulfillment, production, etc.).

- Invite success. Send invitations (including a "show-only" offer and a map to your booth) to everyone on your mailing list. Send press releases.

- Have an objective for going. Attract qualified prospects, sell your products and services, gather names and addresses and other information for your mailing list, or get media coverage. If you don't know why you're there, you'll feel overwhelmed. You should still have an objective even if you're not renting a booth—to connect with possible cross-promotion partners, network with prospects and other experts, and meet representatives of the trade media.

- Design an interesting, interactive display: Have a questionnaire, samples, or a demonstration. Make a special offer at the show. Have refreshments. Stage a publicity event, even if it's just having two friends dressed as ballerinas walking around the show handing out literature about your music boxes. Run a contest.

- Be client-centered. Always. Present the solutions to the client's problems. Emphasize benefits. "Hi. I'm Roberta Wickham. Please feel free to see how I help businesses avoid costly sexual harassment suits."

Be prepared for any orders, requests for information, or other good stuff. Then follow up on every contact you made.

You can also sell at flea markets and swap meets, if your goods are relatively inexpensive and fit well with the product mix already at the market. If your target market goes to swap meets, you can do some selling and get very valuable customer feedback at the same time. Offering refreshments, a demonstration, or a free sample are good ways to ensure your booth gets more than its share of traffic.

SPECIAL REPORTS

Special reports (or tip sheets, booklets, information packets, and so on) are great. They don't cost much to produce, they are a terrific premium or incentive, and they develop your credibility while containing a not-so-subtle sales message. If you can write, or have a friend who can, brainstorm special reports you can offer. One of the best formats is the number list: The Five Toxins in Commercial Baby Food and How to Neutralize Them; Seven Easy Steps to Save at Least $2,500 a Year on College Tuition; Twenty-One Ways Your Business Can Save the Earth and Save a Bundle of Money at the Same Time.

One way to make your special report especially effective is to provide solid information about what the reader should do and why. Use specific copy, like: "Make sure your managers understand what constitutes sexual harassment. Studies show that competent management could have prevented 38 percent of sexual harassment lawsuits, responsible for an average of $108,000 per lawsuit." But don't tell them how. For that, they have to come to you. And your last tip will always be "Consult an Expert," containing information about the benefits of hiring you.

TAG LINE

Which is better?

"So, Jorge, what do you do?"

"Well, I, er, have this thing where I grow organic herbs."

"Oh. That sounds interesting. I grow some oregano myself in my windowboxes."

or

"So, Jorge, what do you do?"

"I help restaurants make delicious food using organic herbs I grow."

"Oh. My brother-in-law works at Chez Pez. Do you know him?"

OK, it's just a bit optimistic to expect that everyone you speak with will have a hot prospect brother-in-law. But the second option is more professional-sounding, presents a benefit (delicious food), and broadens the conversation by making it easy to ask questions (which restaurants, what sort of food, what sorts of herbs). And the cost to you? Five minutes of thought and another five of practice. Include a benefit and a brief description of your target market, and keep it very short.

It'll boost your credibility, make the benefits of business more memorable, and every now and then you *will* find a useful brother-in-law.

TAKE-ONE BOXES

If there are a number of locations or stores that attract your target market, think about using take-one boxes. Put your hard-selling, benefit-rich brochure or flyer in the box, and keep it well-stocked and attractive. You'll reach very hot prospects, you won't spend much money, you'll get increased exposure even to people who see the box and don't take one, and you'll be able to measure results.

TELEMARKETING

There are people who don't mind cold calling. There are also people who don't mind having framing nails hammered into their fleshy parts. The truly awful thing about telemarketing is that it works. Very well. But it doesn't have to be cold calling. In fact, telemarketing can be used to:

- Keep in touch with customers, informing them of new services and up-selling them, making sure they were satisfied, and asking for referrals.

- Contact prospects who've responded to one of your marketing efforts and want more information.

- Follow up on your direct mailings. First, you send a letter describing your offer and saying, "I'll give you a ring next week." Then don't forget to call.

- Cold call. Contact people who've never heard of you before, to set up an appointment, make a sale, or just qualify prospects (ask if they're interested in getting more information about your offer).

Cold calling is always the last telemarketing option. But it gets most of the print, because it's the most painful. And that's why we'll give it the most print, too.

Nonmanipulative cold calling (which is one component of High Probability Selling, called High Probability Prospecting) goes something like this:

- State your offer in 45 words or less, including your salutation and introduction.

- Ask prospects if they want what you're offering, without any saccharine-sweet enticement or charm.

- If they say "yes," ask what they'll do if your offer meets all their needs. If they say anything but "If you meet my needs I'll do business with you," tell them that you don't meet with prospects unless they agree to do business if you can meet all their needs.

- Ask if they want to schedule a meeting.

- End the call if you get a negative answer to any of your questions. Do not try to convince the prospect to buy. Remember: it's a frustrating waste of time and mental effort to attempt to turn a low probability prospect into a High Probability Prospect. It's far more profitable to spend your time with those people who are already High Probability Prospects. Only between 1 and 6 percent of the people you call will be High Probability Prospects. Your job is to find them as efficiently as possible, not to convince anyone else to buy. Don't even suggest an appointment unless the prospect clearly wants what you're selling.

If you're more manipulative than that, try this: *introduce* yourself, mention the *benefits* of doing business with you, mention your *offer*, and ask for *permission* to proceed. Got that? Well, this is what it sounds like:

"Ms. Bassett?"

"Yes."

"Hi, Ms. Bassett, this is Bertie Wooster from Healthy Computer Workers here in Bangor [introduction]. We help companies save money on computer-related work injuries [benefit]. I'm calling because we're offering a free on-site evaluation of computer safety to some local businesses [offer]. Is there any reason you wouldn't want to hear more about our free evaluation? [permission]"

Notice that the permission to proceed is phrased negatively. People want to say "no" to telemarketers. When you phrase your permission to proceed in the negative, they can say no and you can still proceed. Also, if there's a genuine reason why they can't speak at the present, or if they're not interested at all (maybe they don't have any computer work-ers), it gives them a chance to stop you before you get on a roll and annoy them with the interruption.

TESTIMONIALS

Testimonials often make the difference between mild interest and a sale. But they must:

- reinforce a specific benefit, and

- be attributed to a person who's just like the prospect.

You don't want a testimonial that says, "Great service. Really well done! I recommend it." Big deal. You want a testimonial that says, "At first I didn't think you really could help my twelve-year-old black Lab become frisky again. But you did—in just three weeks he's acting healthier and happier than he has in five years. I recommend your ser-vice to anyone who loves an old dog!" Now that's a testimonial.

But it's not enough. It's got to be signed with the full name of someone just like the prospect. If it's signed, "A.U. of Pawtuckett," all that says is that A.U. wasn't confident enough to let you use his name. You want to use his full name. And you want to explain why he's just like the prospect: "Aubrey Upjohn, owner of Zippy, a 12-year-old black Lab who was suffering from arthritis and lethargy."

When you're just starting, it's a bit tough. How do you get tes-timonials about a new service or product? First, try getting testimo-nials about yourself. Ask people who know you to write about the wonderful new-business-related benefits they've gotten from just being in the same room as you. And give away samples of your product or service. Then ask the recipients specific questions about the benefits of your product or service: "How long did it take before you noticed a change in your dog's behavior? What exactly did he do that showed you he was feeling better? In what ways does his new behavior differ from his old behavior?"

And then, once you've been in business for a while, keep on asking for testimonials. At first, you might want to offer a premium to people who fill out a customer survey or questionnaire. But even after your files are bulging with testimonials, keep asking for them, though you may want to ax the premium.

Once you get a testimonial, you should get permission to use it. You can make two copies of each testimonial and send them to the people being quoted, requesting that they sign and return one for your use. Or you can send one copy with a note that says that, if you don't hear from them within thirty or sixty days, you'll assume you have their permission to use the quote.

One last thing: use testimonials liberally. Every time you mention a benefit in a marketing document, you can pop in one or two testimonials to back you up. And because you're going to be incessantly presenting benefits, you'll have testimonials sprinkled throughout everything you produce.

THANKS

Always offer thanks, in person and through the mail. Whenever you get expert advice, make a sale, get a referral, receive an inquiry, or interact with just about anyone in just about any way, thank them. Be genuine, even if you have to fake it. And, ummm, by the way, many thanks for buying this book. And thanks for reading it. And for starting your own business despite all the risk. Thanks.

YOUR MARKETING PLAN

And there you have it—the most effective marketing techniques very little money can buy. You've been noting all the techniques that'll work for you, haven't you? Good. Now you have to make a plan. This is important. If networking seemed like a great way to get your business started without much financial investment, you've got to sit down and plan to network on a regular basis, with very clear objectives, before it will pay off.

If you don't have a fairly complete marketing plan to which you are committed, the payoff is unlikely. You'll attend a networking group a couple of times, and then let it slide because you're not getting immediate results. But remember Levinson's Law of Investment—marketing is an investment, and you don't toss your investment if it doesn't pay off early. Your marketing plan will remind you that you should be attending the weekly meetings this month if you want to be able to ask for referrals next month.

So look at all the marketing techniques you think you ought to use. Evaluate them for cost, ease, and effectiveness.

- "Cost" is easy. If you can't afford an ongoing commitment to run a classified ad in your town's weekly entertainment newspaper, don't even start. Don't look at the cost of a one-time marketing blitz but at a continuing campaign. If you can't afford it for the long haul, move on to the next technique.

- "Ease" is also easy. If you are deathly afraid of public speaking, giving a lecture series—though theoretically a great marketing technique—won't exactly work wonders for you. If you can't get committed to a technique, even though it's affordable, don't use it. And also discard other ideas, such as writing an episode of *Friends* that revolves around your product, that are not much more than impossible dreams.

- "Effectiveness" is not so easy. Sending a series of direct mailings to each of the 900 typewriter repairpeople in your mailing list catalog might be affordable. And it might be easy. But will it be effective? You know what it'll cost you—$1,400 for mailing a letter, two postcards, and making a phone call. But will 5 percent of the market buy your newsletter, *Profitable Typewriter Repair in the Computer Age*? Will 10 percent? Or will you just get 1 percent? If you need an outrageously high response to break even (such as 10 percent), you probably want to drop the idea. But if it's borderline, you want to test it. And if you need just a half of a percent response, you want to take yourself out to dinner.

For techniques that are very low cost, and that you expect to work particularly well with your business, you can assume effectiveness for your marketing plan. If you'll be spending no more than a couple of hours a month and a modest amount of money, and you have a close personal relationship with the perfect cross-promotion partners, you don't have to waste time and effort testing. Just plan to spend those hours and that money every month until your cross-promotion is a profitable, regular source of customers.

Once you've narrowed down the number of techniques you intend to use, make a plan. Your marketing plan should cover every week for at least four to six months and, if you can stand it, even longer. That's not to say that your marketing won't change as you get feedback—it will. You're not locked into a rigid program that won't allow for improvisation or improvement. But don't tinker unnecessarily—commit to your plan until you have definite feedback that one of your marketing techniques failed or that a new one will succeed. Then toss the failure and go with the success, and irrevocably commit to the new plan until you improve that one, too.

Here's a brief sample of a marketing plan for a graphic designer who's combining design and holistic health into a mini-empire. It's pretty simple. You don't want to overwhelm yourself with too much, too soon. But if the following plan is followed, steady, profitable progress will be made. There are also no flashes of genius in the plan. We sketched it out to give you an idea of what the final product could look like. If we were going to use this plan, we'd extend it further into the future. The marketing tasks would get less specific, but we'd still do it to keep ourselves on track. If you can commit to a similar plan, you'll be well on your way to gold and glory.

September

Week 1

Attend meeting of Alternative Health Providers Association. Develop tag line. Collect as many marketing materials as possible. Get membership directory. Time: two hours. Cost: nothing.

Assemble mailing list of healers from their ads in local papers, business cards on bulletin boards, and AHPA membership directory. Time: three hours (including driving around to New Age stores to look at their bulletin boards). Cost: nothing.

Call healers I know, or my friends know, to tell them what I'm doing, ask what they need, get feedback, and ask for referrals to other healers I should talk to. Send thank-you notes and deep discount coupon (remember to get testimonials after they use service). Time: an hour and a half. Cost: $8 for thank-you notes and postage.

Week 2

Speak to that psychic woman about developing a line of customized, psychic-developed business cards. Call them Psychic Designs? Great press-release fodder in addition to a possible extra-income source. Time: one hour. Cost: nothing.

Talk to the editor at the local weekly paper about a monthly column on alternative healing in the community. Time: half an hour. Cost: nothing.

Write tip sheet on How to Make Money Like a Capitalist and Still Live Like a Healer. Time: four or five hours. Cost: nothing.

Continue assembling mailing list. Time: probably not more than another hour or two. Cost: nothing.

Call the referrals I got from healers last week. Ask them same questions and for even more referrals. Time: one or two hours. Cost: nothing.

Week 3

Write sample *Fresno Healing* column and send to editor. Time: three to four hours (interviewing a healer and writing 700-word column). Cost: nothing.

Talk to printer about costs of printing quarterly directory of local healers. Research what similar publications charge for advertising. Ask healer friends if they'd pay whatever cost turns out to be necessary for me to make at least $700 per month on directory. Time: three hours. Cost: $10 in long-distance charges to call similar publications.

Write and send letter with sample business card to local healers on assembled list. Offer 20 percent off makeover of all their marketing materials. Time: four to five hours. Cost: $120.

Week 4

Call editor regarding column. Time: half an hour. Cost: nothing.

Return calls generated from letter re: marketing makeover. Time: who knows? Hopefully a couple of hours at least. Cost: nothing.

Call referrals from healers that I got two weeks ago. Ask same questions all over again. Time: one hour. Cost: nothing.

Check *Associations in Print* for associations of healers who publish newsletters. Contact them re: marketing materials column, showing before and after examples from members who write in. Time: two hours. Cost: nothing.

Track responses from letter. Time: one hour. Cost: nothing.

October

Week 5

Attend Alternative Health Providers meeting. Give tips about how marketing materials can improve income. Ask about interest re: a quarterly directory of healers. Time: two hours. Cost: nothing.

Write and send press releases to business and New Age magazines and newsletters about psychic designs. Time: four hours. Cost: $50.

Send follow-up postcard to local healers who haven't called. Time: two hours. Cost: $45.

Week 6

Contact local healing schools (massage, hypnotherapy, etc.) offering to lead a short seminar for new grads about making marketing materials. Time: hour and a half. Cost: nothing.

Call healers re: post card offer. Time: four hours. Cost: nothing (local calls).

And so on. (And when you're done, don't forget to plug the costs of your marketing into your business plan.)

That's a pretty informal plan. But after just six weeks, the business owner has assembled a mailing list, sent two direct mail packages, telemarketed, networked at an association, asked for referrals, explored the possibility of starting a directory, written and sent press releases for an unusual and promotable business extension, worked on getting a holistic healing column in the local paper and a marketing column in national healing newsletters, tried to arrange seminars, and developed a tip sheet. If she keeps up marketing at this pace, she'll be doing much, much more than any comparable business, and making that much more money, too.

Whenever a holistic health practitioner in her town needs a designer, he'll think of her first—because she keeps her name in front of him. She's already working on expanding her market through columns in national newsletters and a very promotable product—business cards developed collaboratively with a psychic. (By the way, even if she doesn't make a whole lot of money on the psychic-designed cards, she'll definitely get publicity if she targets the right media. And that publicity will pay off many times over when she includes it in all her other marketing materials. Media coverage provides much credibility, and credibility leads to sales.)

The key here—and the reason for having a written marketing plan—is consistency and completeness. Don't get yourself in an uproar about including every little thing you do and every minute and dollar that it takes to do it. Just develop a plan that will work for you, that will remind you to do all the marketing you need to make your business a success. Then do that marketing.

And then, once you start raking in all that cash, you're home free, right? Sure. Except for two little things...bookkeeping and taxes.

The Quick and Easy Guide to Accounting and Taxes

PART FOUR

Bookkeeping and Taxes

BOOKKEEPING AND TAXES rank right up there with public speaking, disembowelment, and cold calling when it comes to Things People Would Rather Avoid. And we, too, hate them. But as your always-smilin' authors, we're obliged to put on a happy face. So here's the good news: 8 percent of all the taxes you pay actually goes to good stuff!, and bookkeeping is an extremely valuable business tool that's pretty easy once you get the hang of it.

Because we believe in putting off taxes as long as possible, we'll discuss bookkeeping first.

Bookkeeping isn't that bad. Really. The reason bookkeeping gets such a bad rap is because it's all about numbers, the IRS makes you do it, and it's full of incomprehensible gibberish such as amortization, accrual, and accounts due—and that's only the "A's".

Fair enough, that stuff *is* awful. But bookkeeping is far less awful when you understand how to do it, and when someone gives you a quick-and-easy method for effective record keeping. We'll do that. And it can be positively inspiring when you use your records as a business planning tool. Your records provide you with a snapshot of the condition of your business. Just a snapshot, mind you—there are more important considerations in the long-term health of your business than your financials, such as your creativity, perseverance, and desperation to succeed. Still, an objective snapshot can be tremendously helpful.

And even if you're a slovenly wretch in every other way, keeping good records is imperative for your continued mental well-being. Why? Because the alternative is truly appalling—pouring your blood, sweat, and tears into your business and not knowing if the money you have in the bank is yours, if you're making more than $6 per hour, if you can afford to pay the phone bill, if your expenses are twice what they were three months ago, if.... You get the idea.

We kept decent records while running our computer imaging business, but there was still a month when we did fairly well, and were busily congratulating ourselves until we discovered that, because our records hadn't been updated, about half of our monthly income was eaten up by unexpected expenses. That is not even a little bit fun. All record keeping takes is a couple of hours a week and another couple at the end of the month—not a high price for the information you get.

Remember all those educated guesses you made in your business plan, trying to determine if your business was financially feasible? Now your books will show you that you guessed well, or will provide early warning that you have to raise prices, lower expenses, or sell more before you can make a profit.

The other big reason to keep books well is that if you maintain professional-quality books, even if the numbers are pathetically small, you feel that you're running a professional-quality business. Keeping all your receipts in a pizza box doesn't exactly enhance self-confidence.

OK, we've sold you on the necessity of bookkeeping. And here are some of bookkeeping's basic rules:

- Always keep your personal money and your business money separate. Have a bank account and checkbook exclusively for business use.

- Pay for all your business expenses with checks. It makes documenting your expenses much easier.

- Deposit all your business income into the business account.

- Pay yourself a "wage" (personal or proprietor's draw) out of the business account. If you need business money for some personal reason, first withdraw it as a personal draw (by writing a check to yourself), and then use it. Don't pay for the personal expense directly from the business account.

And one last tip: banks, although pretty much uniformly awful, are also all different. Don't just get an account at the closest bank. Shop around.

Now to the nitty-gritty. There are two kinds of bookkeeping and two accounting methods.

First, there's single-entry bookkeeping and double-entry bookkeeping. Double-entry bookkeeping is better in every way, except that it's tremendously confusing, overwhelming, and miserable. Quite frankly, we have no idea how to do double-entry bookkeeping. We don't *want* to know how to do it. We have a hard enough time remembering how to do single-entry bookkeeping, which is plenty good enough for us. It will probably be plenty good enough for you, too. The only exception to our rule against using double-entry bookkeeping is when you're using accounting software on your computer—that'll do double-entry automatically, so it's no hassle at all.

Then there are two accounting methods: the cash method and the accrual method. The difference between the two methods is very simple. When you use the cash method, income is recorded when you actually get money, and expenses are recorded when you actually spend money. In the accrual method, income is recorded when you earn it, and expenses are recorded when you incur them. So with accrual, you record income when you bill a client (not when you actually get the money), and you record an expense when you order supplies (not when you actually pay for them). The accrual method basically counts promises to pay or be paid as real money.

The cash method certainly does seem much simpler, doesn't it? Well that's too bad, because the cash method can only be used by those businesses that do not maintain an inventory. If you stock and sell any *thing*, you've absolutely got to use accrual. Why? Because the IRS says so, that's why.

However, if you have a pure service business and don't sell any related stuff, you can use the cash method. But because we encourage you to find stuff to sell (because you've already got a client with an open wallet, and you should provide him with the best stuff as well as the best service), you'll probably be using the accrual method.

Great, but how do you use either method?

Before we started our first business, we read sixteen books about bookkeeping. For our efforts, we became terminally confused. And it's not as if we were dabbling in the waters of high finance. We just wanted to know how to keep track of:

- how much we were spending and where we were spending it

- how much we were bringing in and how we were earning it

- how the business was doing (Were we making or losing money? Were we spending a disproportionate amount of money on an unnecessary expense?)

- we wanted to comply with the law that a small business keep complete records for tax purposes.

So here's our easy-as-possible guide to bookkeeping (and in only seven words): *Buy a bookkeeping system and use it.*

Bookkeeping systems are prefab record-keeping books for small businesses. They explain everything you have to do, have pre-labeled columns and a couple of sample pages, and are so well put together they do most of the work for you. You can buy one at any office supply store. They usually cost about $15. Don't get the $4.95 receipt book instead, and then wonder what we're talking about. If it costs much less than $15, it's the wrong thing.

If you sit down with your bookkeeping system for twenty minutes after you buy it, you'll almost certainly get the hang of what you're supposed to write and where you're supposed to write it. If you sit down with it for a couple of minutes every few days or every week, and then an hour or two every month, you will have something better—a deep and abiding understanding of your business. And you'll have a more profitable business as well.

We've used the *IDEAL Weekly Bookkeeping and Tax Record* and have been quite happy with it. We've also heard good things about the DOME system. And as they seem to be the only two systems generally available, you should do OK. Both IDEAL and DOME make specific systems for particular businesses, but you'll probably want the "general" system of weekly bookkeeping, and that works great.

You may be shocked and appalled that we didn't recommend that you buy small business software and do all your record-keeping on your computer. This may be nothing more than Luddite lunacy, but we think that for at least the first three months, you ought to keep your books on paper. There are two reasons we don't encourage you to *start* with bookkeeping software:

1. Writing things down in a little book with everything carefully explained isn't such a burden. You can do it.

2. We think that the act of writing stuff down and figuring it out keeps you in better touch with your business. It is easier to understand how all those little numbers add up to success or failure. Accounting software makes bookkeeping so simple that you don't really have to know how the different columns of numbers relate—which is exactly what you ought to know.

Having said that, small business record-keeping software is excellent. You won't make any math errors, it'll do double-entry record-keeping for you automatically, and you can add up all the expenses or income from a specific area at the touch of a button. Generating a variety of reports is a breeze. If your business is more complex than any of ours have been—if you have a fairly extensive inventory or lots of assets to depreciate—you'll want to computerize as soon as possible. If your business is simple or you don't own a computer, don't worry. For a truly small business, all you really need is a bookkeeping system, a pencil, and a calculator.

To prepare you for the awesome responsibility of using your bookkeeping system, here's an overview of what you'll be doing with it:

INCOME

Whenever you make a sale, you keep a record of that sale on an invoice, receipt, or cocktail napkin.

If you only rarely make sales, you can use a customized invoice written on your letterhead. Include the date, customer's name and address, a description of the service or product, and the amount, and show sales tax separately. Make two, and keep one for your records. And, of course, use the invoice as a marketing tool. In addition to reiterating your guarantee, discount for pre-payment, and so forth, use your invoice to make an offer to the newly gained customer.

If you are making more regular sales, buy an invoice book—you know, one of those little books of receipts that many small businesses use. Make sure you buy one that provides you with a duplicate of each transaction, and fill out all of the information indicated, remembering to show sales tax separately.

Then you're half done. During your next regularly scheduled book-keeping session, record your sales in your books. Unless you have a relatively high volume of sales, you probably don't need to do your bookkeeping every day. Every three days, or even once a week, can be fine. The goal is to avoid a huge backlog of receipts and to keep on top of your financial situation. If you can do that while posting once a week, great.

But definitely run a monthly total at the end of every month. There'll be a form in your bookkeeping system for this. Use it monthly to see if you made money, lost money, or broke even, and why.

At the end of the year, add up all the monthly totals and you've got what's known as the yearly total. Neat, huh? If you're using the accrual method, that's all there is to it. If you're using the cash method, make sure you don't include all those sales you've made but haven't been paid for yet. Put them aside in a little folder that says "accounts receivable," and then add them in to the new year when they (finally) get paid.

CREDIT

If you sell on credit, you'll make more sales. And you'll probably make more money, too. Even after subtracting deadbeats and administrative costs, you'll usually come out ahead. But it's a hassle. You've got to abide by credit and lending laws, figure out payment timetables and finance charges, have a collection system, and develop some way of deciding how much credit to give. If offering credit is one of your big benefits, or if it's standard in your field, you've got to keep a credit ledger as well as an income ledger—and you need more information than we can provide here. Read the books we recommend in the Resource section.

The easy way to extend credit, and the only way we can recommend, is through a credit card. Unfortunately, your bank probably won't give you a credit card merchant account, which you need to accept plastic. Banks don't like giving merchant accounts to home-based or otherwise tiny businesses. If you're starting a retail store or are renting an office and have a relationship with the bank and a good credit history, you might get lucky. But you'll probably have to get a merchant account through a less rigid, more expensive source. There are companies that will get you a merchant account and lease you a credit card terminal, but it'll cost you. They take a higher percentage of each sale and charge more for terminals than banks do, but they may be the only ones who'll work with you. Look in any of the business opportunity magazines or online entrepreneur newsgroups, because they usually have ads for companies that give merchant accounts to home-based businesses, or drop us a line and we'll let you know if we've found a good one.

EXPENSES

Sometimes there's no getting around it: you've got to spend money on business-related expenses. When it happens, use a check. Get a receipt. File the receipt. Enter the amount in the proper category in your bookkeeping system or software. On those very rare occasions when you pay for a business expense with cash, record it immediately. Your half of the tax game is to make sure that you never pay for anything without recording it as a business expense. If you pay for business stuff with a credit card, pay off the appropriate expenses on your credit card bill with your business checkbook and record them in the proper category.

The proper category could be almost anything. The bookkeeping system you bought has some preprinted categories—rent, utilities, payroll, supplies, inventory, insurance, advertising—which will probably work fine for you. If you want to add a new one, just cross out payroll or whatever else you won't be using and write in the new category. If you're using "miscellaneous" more than any other category, you either need some new categories or you don't understand that buying paper clips ought to go in "supplies." Whichever it is, stop it already.

As with your income, you'll need to figure your total monthly expenses. You do this by adding the weekly expenses together. See how easy that is. You'll also want to generate a year-end expenses summary. This isn't tricky either. The only thing about it that's worth mentioning is how to deal with accrual accounting. All the bills that you haven't yet paid and all the expenses you've incurred but haven't yet been billed for should be listed in your books and marked "accounts payable." Even though you'll actually be paying for them next year, they are deductible only for the year just ended. Make sure you don't list them twice.

ASSETS

You probably don't have much in the way of assets. There's your cash, checking account, your savings account, and your inventory, if you even have that much (more likely, you just have one or two of the above).

As we said above, if you have to track much inventory, or the depreciation of your business equipment, your recordkeeping will get a bit more complex.

For inventory, you'll either need an inventory ledger (tracking what you have, what and when you ordered, what and when you received, and what and when you paid), or inventory-control software. For a very small business, it's probably best to have very little inventory, and to reorder often. You never want to make a customer wait for an order, but you don't want to put all your pizza money into inventory, either.

For depreciation, you'll need to do some more reading. Recovery periods and depreciation rates differ and change all the time. Those easy-to-read-and-understand pamphlets the IRS puts out will explain in more detail, as will small business books devoted exclusively to bookkeeping.

But the bottom line is this: if you bought office furniture, equipment, business machinery, business buildings, or business vehicles, you don't claim the entire cost all at once. Actually, you can claim up to $17,500 in the year of purchase, but we recommend you claim a portion of the value over a number of years in order to make the most of the tax deduction. So if you buy a $150 cash register, instead of claiming $150 this year, you claim $15 a year for ten years—the actual amount and length of time varies. Our IDEAL bookkeeping system has a special page for this, and many software programs deal with it relatively simply. But relative simplicity is still painfully confusing in the case of depreciation. You probably won't run into a big depreciation snag because you can't afford those expensive purchases anyhow—but if you do, buy a small-business accounting book, run to the nearest SCORE (Service Corps of Retired Executives) office, ask at your Chamber of Commerce if there are any free workshops, find an accountant you can afford or barter with, and cross your fingers.

If you want more information about small business bookkeeping, there are many good books out there on the subject. *Small Time Operator* by Bernard Kamoroff is the classic. There are several financial reports that accountant types recommend small businesses run periodically—such as profit and loss analyses and cash flow projections. Running them would undoubtedly help you understand the financial condition of your business. But they're nothing to worry about when you're starting a business with six hundred dollars, a toothpaste tube, and a box of thumbtacks. Our advice is that you don't bother until you get big enough to actually have a respectable profit, loss, and cash flow.

TAXES

The reason to pay taxes is simple: If you don't do it, the IRS can squash you like a bug.

The goal is to pay as little in taxes as *legally* possible. We definitely don't recommend taking too much money under the table or otherwise lying on your taxes. Not for karmic reasons either. If the IRS does find out that you've been less than forthright about your income, you'll wish you'd declared that $700 you thought would slip by. For the pathetic amount of money you'll be saving, it's simply not worth the risk. Having your business and your life pawed over, prodded, and squeezed by humorless federal drones makes paper-cutting your eye look like good, clean fun. Don't cheat.

But do pay as little tax as possible by deducting as much as possible. All your business expenses are deductible. Keep track of them, and deduct them.

Expenses you incur before you actually start your business may or may not be deductible. So start your business *very* small. Make one, insignificant sale to a friend to prove you're in business. Then buy whatever startup materials you need—it's all deductible, as now you're an established business.

The Home Office Deduction

The rules for deducting part of your rent when you have a home office or work space change a little every year. As of right now, you can deduct that portion of your rent that you spend on business space if your home office is the primary place you conduct your business and if it is a separate, identifiable space regularly and exclusively used for business.

If you only work at home, you're set. Otherwise, there are two tests to decide if your home office is the primary place you conduct business. First, do you spend the majority of your work time there? This is an easy numerical test—if you spend more work time at home than anywhere else, you pass. Second, is your work in the home office the most important, consequential, or influential work you do for your business? Let's say you run your catering business out of your home office, and rent a commercial kitchen for cooking. You'd probably be denied the home office deduction even if you spend seventy percent of your time in the office, because your business is fundamentally about cooking, which you do elsewhere. The same goes for any business for which the income-producing work happens at another location.

You cannot use your kitchen table as office space and get the home office deduction. You've got to use a space that is separate from the rest of the house—a spare bedroom converted into an office, or even a corner of a room that is somehow sectioned off from the rest of the room. Just make sure your work space is visibly set apart and is exclusively used for business.

If you satisfy these requirements, figure out what percentage of your apartment or house is taken up by your home office, and multiply that by your annual rent and utility payment. That's how much you can deduct for your home office. If you're genuinely not sure if you satisfy the requirements as a home office, you can either take the deduction and cross your fingers or call the IRS for more information.

Sole Proprietorships

If you have a sole proprietorship, you and your business are one entity. Business profits and losses are filed on your personal tax return. First you fill out a Schedule C or C-EZ. But you can only file a Schedule C-EZ if you had:

- between $0-$25,000 income

- under $2,000 in expenses

- only one sole proprietorship, and

- no inventory, employees, or depreciation.

If you have more than one sole proprietorship, you have to file one Schedule C for each of them, and then include all that information on your 1040.

The Schedule C or C-EZ records your business income and expenses and shows what your business net profit or loss is. Then you plug that number into your personal return and add it to your income from all other sources and are taxed at whatever tax bracket you end up in.

Sounds pretty easy, doesn't it? Sure it is. Unless you make at least $400 in profit. Then you have to make "estimated tax" payments to the IRS, using form 1040-ES. They're required four times a year. In equal payments on April 15, June 15, September 15, and January 15. (You don't have to send in the fourth payment separately if you file your tax return by January 31 and pay the balance due.) But how do you know how much tax you'll owe before the year is over? You don't. So what you do is base your payment on the amount of tax you paid last year, even though you weren't in business. Divide your previous year's total tax payment by four, and send it to the IRS in quarterly installments.

Partnership

If you have a general partnership (which is the business type you'll probably have if working solo isn't for you), filing taxes is more complex than for a sole proprietorship. Still, there are similarities: each partner is responsible for all liabilities of the business, and you report business profit or loss on your personal tax return.

But the partnership itself, although it doesn't pay taxes, is a legal entity and must file an annual tax return (Form 1065). After the partnership files the 1065, each partner must file a Schedule K-1. This tells the IRS how much money *you* made from the partnership. You could have taken 50 percent of the profit or loss, or any other percentage (just make sure all your partners know how much everyone gets before starting the business). A partnership can be divided up any way you want. (You can even have two partners who each own half of a business divide the profit up differently) The K-1 tells how much of the partnership's profit or loss was allocated to you. This information then goes onto your personal 1040 return. With a partnership, as with a sole proprietorship, you've got to pay quarterly estimated tax payments. Use the 1040-ES, guess what you'll make or lose (base your payments on your last year's payment), and pay your estimated taxes.

That's the brief, introductory course on taxes for partnerships. This is one reason we encourage sole proprietorships. But if you've got your heart set on a partnership, read up on the tax laws in one of the books we recommend in the resources section.

CORPORATIONS, S CORPORATIONS, LIMITED LIABILITY COMPANIES

Oddly enough, paying taxes for these more complex types of business is easy. Hire a tax pro. Pay what and when they tell you to pay.

Payroll Taxes

If you need to hire people, do it the easy way: rent employees through an employment agency, even if they'll be working for you for a while. Yes, we know that temp services are evil. But payroll taxes and employment laws are even more evil. You'll pay more per hour, but the agency will withhold taxes, do payroll reporting, be liable for legal screw-ups, and offer a pension plan and benefits. If you ever become a large small business, you might want to do all this stuff in-house. Until that glorious day arrives, do it the easy way.

You Win Some, and...

If your business is a sole proprietorship or a partnership, you can write off business losses on your individual tax return. So if you've kept your job and started a money-losing business on the side, you can deduct the business losses from the job income. And it gets better. If you lose more in your business than your total income, you can carry the loss back into the tax return you filed three years ago and get a refund now. If you lost more than you made this year and three years ago, carry the loss back into the return you filed two years ago. Still more loss? Apply it to last year's tax return. And if you're the King or Queen of All Losers, and have still more loss to claim, you can apply it to future years—up to fifteen years in the future.

Of course, you probably won't be taking a loss at all and can't recover all that money you paid to the IRS over the past three years. Pity. And even if you do take a loss, it'll probably be pretty small. Although we're not going to explain how to fill out the IRS forms for a Net Operating Loss Carry-Over, we thought you'd like to know that if you do lose your shirt, you might be able to get a little cash back.

But we hope you have to pay tax. Lots of tax. Tens of thousands of dollars every quarter. And while you do, we hope you still remember your terrifying, thrilling first steps toward starting your own business and creating your own life.

You're in Business!

YIKES. **T**HIS IS ALMOST THE END OF THE BOOK, which means you'll have to actually start working pretty soon. We'll help you put it off a little longer, though, 'cause we like you.

So here you are. You've developed a business based on your guiding principle, a business plan to help you run the business, and a marketing plan to bring in the money. You know about paying your taxes and keeping your books.

Now you've got to actually make those phone calls, write those sales letters, and borrow that money from your rich uncle. This is where all the dreaming—our favorite part of starting a business—collides with reality, which is not always our favorite part. This will almost certainly be hard. Starting your own business, even when you love the work, is tough. It's all *you*. There's no one else to blame when you act like an imbecile, when your grandiose expectations fall flat, when you don't know the answer to an easy question, when you offer the wrong advice or are rude for no reason. There's no one to tell you what to do when you're staring into the fridge, trying to get motivated.

So, although it's New Age-y, here's an affirmation that may help:

Every day, in every way, working for myself is better than being an insignificant drone in someone else's suffocating, ugly, and unremittingly stupid business.

We love positive affirmations.

So running your own business is tough. So what? It's *yours*. How many people do you know who hate their jobs? Who get a stomachache every Sunday night just thinking about having to return to work? Who hate the companies that steal their lives for $9 per hour? And who bitch about their pay, their work, their bosses, their coworkers, and the rest of their deflated dreams well into the second six-pack?

We've been there, and we imagine you have, too. And these people have our sympathy. But they can just shut up already.

They haven't taken the risk you will take. They won't lay it all on the line, or spend money they can't afford in order to follow their dream. They won't be rejected six times in an hour just to get to the seventh person. They won't stand at that point where research and planning end, and take the leap into what could be the most rewarding personal success, or the most depressing failure.

And that's what you're about to do. At some point, the kind of business you start and how much success you have just doesn't matter. What really matters is that you took the risk. You did it. You didn't just whine about having a better life. You busted your butt to make your life better.

Think about the bosses you've had. Check out the smartly dressed businesspeople at the next table at the coffee shop. You are smarter than they are. You, in fact, *can* find your ass with both hands. You have a clue. Sure, you don't have any money. And despite the close attention you paid to the accounting chapter, you're still not quite sure what in the hell "accrual" means, anyway. And you've got a goofy business that will appeal to a niche market so tightly targeted that you know both of the members by name. But you can do it. And if you need a hand along the way, drop us a line. Our address is P.O. Box 2066, Santa Barbara, CA 93120. Our e-mail address is GenerateE@AOL.com. We'd give you our phone number, but the truth is that despite our stunning success as authors and entrepreneurs, a stable life still eludes us and we tend to move into a different telephone prefix every year or so.

Listen: you've plowed through this whole book. You know more about starting a small business than almost anyone else in your situation. All it takes now is doing it. Start small. Make a couple of sales. Keep plugging away. Follow our wise advice, and you'll end up with a thriving small business. You'll have the money you need and the lifestyle you love. Imagine that day when you're doing what you love to do, and getting what you need to live. You *have a life*. You're not waiting to be discovered or to sell out. You've made your life, and you built it from nothing. Be proud.

APPENDIX

The "We Practice What We Preach" Pages

Here's our irresistible offer:

Send us your marketing plan for evaluation, and we guarantee you'll make an additional $1,000 in your first year in business if you follow our recommendations. That's right:

We'll Give Your Marketing Plan a Tuneup, and We'll Pay You $1,000 If Our Advice Doesn't Add $1,000 to Your Bottom Line

You've already developed a powerhouse of a marketing plan. But it's hard to be objective about your own work. Is it as good as it can be? Is it complete? Is it practical? Is it a money magnet?

Maybe you're making unrealistic assumptions. Maybe your cunning plan is doomed to failure for some obscure reason. Maybe your plan is almost there, but needs a little extra work or some expert feedback. Or maybe you're right on target.

Whatever the current state of your marketing plan, you can always use an unbiased evaluation. And more than that, you can really use practical suggestions that are guaranteed to increase your profits. And we've got 'em.

Just send us your marketing plan, business description, and your favorite resources and we'll provide suggestions, ideas, modifications, and even leads to specific resources if appropriate.

And if our advice doesn't lead to an additional $1,000 the first year you're in business, we'll pay you $1,000. All you have to do is show that you consistently followed our wise advice, and if it resulted in only a trifling $999 or less, we'll give you a grand.

225

But it'll cost you. Actually, it'll only cost you $99. Think about it: If you follow our advice, and it doesn't generate over ten times what you pay us within one year, we'll give you over ten times your money back. Ow! Now that's a guarantee.

Does that qualify as an irresistible offer? We hope so.

But why are we risking a thousand dollars to offer the marketing plan Tune-Up?

- We love ideas, and we love marketing. Sitting around and reading marketing plans all day is our kind of fun.

- We want you on our mailing list. We're working to develop all sorts of offers that will help your small business—but we can't share them with you unless we know where you live.

- We're going to try to up-sell you. Well, of course we are. We've read this book, too, you know.

- If our advice doesn't make you a thousand dollars, we suck. Creating and improving marketing plans is what we're good at. If you follow our advice for a year and don't make much more than $1,000, we ought to be working as peep show janitors, not marketing consultants.

So send your business description, marketing plan, and $99 (payable to Naftali Marketing) to P.O. Box 2066, Santa Barbara, CA 93120. Or if you've got a question about this offer, mail it to us at that address or e-mail us at GenerateE@AOL.com.

Resources

Our Favorite Book

You may have noticed that we love ideas. If ideas and creativity light your bulb too, we enthusiastically recommend *Thinkertoys: A Handbook of Business Creativity for the '90s* by Michael Michalko (Ten Speed Press). It's a fantastic resource for generating and refining ideas. And not only business-related ideas—you can apply Michalko's techniques to any creative problem. We're cheap and almost never buy a book if we can check it out of the library—this book is one of the few exceptions.

Find Your Passion

Our "Find Your Guiding Principle" chapter was stolen from about seven books, and then repeatedly submitted to and modified by various slacker friends until they were satisfied with the results. The books that are most responsible for the final product, and that we recommend if you want to do more self-exploration, are:

The Truth About You by Arthur F. Miller and Ralph T. Mattson (Ten Speed Press). This is the most complete find-your-passion book that we've found. If you want to dig deeper into your guiding principle, this is the first book you ought to buy.

I Could Do Anything If Only I Knew What It Was: Discover What You Really Want and How to Get It by Barbara Sher and Barbara Smith (New York: Dell, 1995). This book contains many exercises and much wise advice to help you find out what you want to do with your life. It has a more psychological approach than we offered: if you want to stop stumbling over your psyche on the road to success, we very much recommend you read it.

What Color Is Your Parachute? by Richard N. Bolles (Ten Speed Press, annual). If you're one of the seventeen people on the planet who haven't heard of this book, here's all you need to know: for over two and a half decades this book has remained the preeminent source of career-finding wisdom. Although it's oriented toward getting a job, it is also a great resource for the budding entrepreneur. Buy it, use it, and benefit from it.

Do It! Let's Get Off Our Butts by Peter McWilliams and John-Roger (Prelude Press, 1994). Despite the cultish influence, there's good information, motivation, and quotation in this book. Just ignore the final two pages that try to sell you on J-R's organizations.

Mind Mapping

We presented a simplified version of mind mapping: no colors, no pictures, no bursts of creative genius. In fact, mind mapping is much more interesting and helpful than the abridged version we presented in this book. If you want the whole enchilada, check out the following:

Mindmapping: Your Personal Guide to Exploring Creativity and Problem-Solving by Joyce Wycoff (New York: Berkley Publications, 1991). This is a friendly and helpful guide to the uses and techniques of mindmapping. It's quite accessible and covers everything you need to know to use mindmapping effectively for brainstorming, problem-solving, decision-making, and prioritizing.

The Mind Map Book: How to Use Radiant Thinking to Maximize Your Brain's Untapped Potential by Tony Buzan and Barry Buzan (New York: NAL-Dutton, 1996). Tony Buzan developed mindmapping and in this challenging and stimulating book he explains it. It's more advanced (and colorful) than Wycoff's book—if you read hers and were hungry for more, this should satisfy your appetite.

Business Idea Directories

If you just couldn't get enough of the Business Idea Directory, there are many books that list businesses you can start. We should warn you, though, that many of the ideas they contain are boring (such as medical claims processing), silly (such as making apple dolls), expensive (such as being a commodities broker), or unlikely (such as being a professional Abraham Lincoln look-alike). You're probably better off just browsing at the bookstore with a notebook in your hand than actually spending money on most of them.

But there are also guides to starting up a business in specific areas of interest: animals, gourmet foods, farming, plants, computers, crafts, the environment, arts, etc. Many of these are very good. There are too many to list here, though, and we'd probably overlook the one book that fits perfectly with your dream business. So if you're interested in more information about a particular business area, however obscure, the chances are that a book exists to tell you more. If you can't find it in the obvious places, check Books in Print for the subject of your desire or the classified ads of a magazine aimed at the appropriate market.

Market Research

There aren't any great market research books aimed specifically at the very small-time entrepreneur. But the following three books come close. They all cover the basics of market research, though probably in more detail that you'll want. Still, they're the best books for the beginner.

Market Research Toolbox: A Concise Guide for Beginners by Edward McQuarrie (Thousand Oaks, Calif.: Sage Publications, 1996).

Look Before You Leap: Market Research Made Easy by Don Doman, et al. (Bellingham, Wash.: Self-Counsel Press, 1993).

Do-It-Yourself Marketing Research by George Breen and A. B. Blankenship (McGraw-Hill).

Marketing

If you're serious about creating a money-making marketing plan, and don't much care who knows it, Jeffrey Lant is the way to go. If you want more information about his books or services, call his Cambridge, Massachusetts publishing company, JLA Publications, at (617) 547-6372, and ask for his catalog.

For copywriting, try *Cash Copy: How to Offer Your Products and Services So Your Prospects Buy Them.... Now!* (1992). If you want to learn how to use copywriting to motivate prospects to buy, you must read this book.

For a complete discussion of marketing, read *Money-Making Marketing: Finding the People Who Need What You're Selling and Making Sure They Buy It* (1996). This book covers marketing research, getting leads, publicity, creating ads, telemarketing, direct mail, and much more.

And for publicity and self-promotion, you need *The Unabashed Self-Promoter's Guide: What Every Man, Woman, Child, and Organization in America Needs to Know about Getting Ahead by Exploiting the Media* (1992). It discusses how to create publicity documents, produce articles, handle interviews, extend the life of your publicity, and many other aspects of self-promotion. This book also includes an extensive list of media directories.

Another excellent discussion of publicity can be found in Marcia Yudjkin's *Six Steps to Free Publicity and Dozens of Other Ways to Win Free Media Attention for You or Your Business* (New York: NAL-Dutton, 1994). It offers clear, lively advice explaining how you can profit from free media coverage.

Jay Conrad Levinson's books are also must-reads. We recommend that you start with plain old *Guerrilla Marketing for the Nineties (1993)* or *The Guerrilla Marketing Handbook* (with Seth Godin, 1994). For info on selling, try *Guerrilla Selling* by Levinson with Bill Gallagher (1991), all published by Houghton Mifflin. There are about ten more books in the Guerrilla Marketing series. They're all good, but there is some repetition, so skim before you buy to make sure you haven't read it all before.

Streetsmart Marketing by Jeff and Marc Slutsky (New York: Wiley, 1989) is a marketing resource that was written with retail businesses in mind, but has fantastic ideas for small home-based businesses as well. There are some clever and low-cost marketing ideas in this book that we haven't seen anywhere else.

Our biggest recommendation for you if you'll be doing much selling is to buy Jacques Werth and Nicholas Ruben's *High Probability Selling* (Langhorne, Penn.: Abba Publishing Company. Call them at 800-394-7762 if you can't find the book in a bookstore near you). It's the best book on nonmanipulative selling that we know of.

There are far too many books about online marketing. Pick the most recent one you can find. Browse through it. If it gives you very specific advice, it's probably worth a longer look. We liked Alfred and Emily

Glossbrenner's *Making Money on the Internet* (Blue Ridge Summit, Penn.: TAB Books, 1995), but it's outdated by now. There's a 1996 version out called *Making More Money on the Internet* (New York: McGraw-Hill) but we haven't seen it yet and so can't recommend it. If it's as good as their first, though, it's worth your consideration.

Word of Mouth Marketing by Jerry Wilson (New York: Wiley, 1994) does a great job explaining how to start and run a business that encourages, and profits from, positive word of mouth.

How to Win Customers and Keep Them for Life by Michael LeBouef (New York: Berkeley Publications, 1989) is a very thorough discussion of customer service. Extremely important and very well presented.

Targeted Public Relations: *How to Get Thousands of Dollars of Free Publicity for Your Product, Service, Organization, or Idea* by Bob Bly (New Jersey: Henry Holt, 1994) is a very straightforward and useful guide to, well, getting thousands of dollars of free publicity for your product, service, organization, or idea. Bly also writes great books about direct mail and how to making money writing.

Bookkeeping and Taxes

For bookkeeping and taxes, the classic is *Small Time Operator* by Bernard Kamoroff (Laytonville, Calif.: Bell Springs Publishing, 1996). It covers everything you need to know about a subject you'd probably rather know nothing about and does it as painlessly as possible.

General Business

Barbara Winter's *Making a Living without a Job: Winning Ways for Creating Work That You Love* (New York: Bantam Books, 1993) is a friendly, "new age-y" guide to starting your own business. It's easy reading and full of good advice.

Homemade Money: How to Select, Start, Manage, Market, and Multiply the Profits of a Business at Home by Barbara Brabec (Cincinnati: Betterway Books, 1994) offers an overview of basically everything for the home-based business.

Running a One-Person Business by Claude Whitmeyer and Salli Rasberry (Ten Speed Press, 1994) is a highly recommended resource for people starting up one-person businesses.

Web Resources

New small business websites are popping up like toadstools after a summer rain. And many of them have toadstool lifespans, too. But here are some websites that are around to stay, or that often update their links to other entrepreneurial websites.

SCORE (Service Corps of Retired Executives) Online
(http://www.scn.org/civic/score-online/)

This is a very well done website that includes the e-mail addresses of SCORE counselors who will help you one-on-one with your small business questions.

Small Business Administration Online
(http://www.sbaonline.sba.gov)

Not only does the SBA Online site contain information about starting and running your small business, but it offers hundreds of small business shareware programs for you to download.

IRS
(http://www.irs.ustreas.gov/prod/cover/html)

A surprisingly friendly website that has more than you want to know about taxes, forms, regulations, and everything else tax-related.

Smallbiz Net
(http://www.lowe.org/smbiznet/)

This site has a great online resources section, website reviews, and many worthwhile links.

National Association for the Self-Employed
(http://selfemployed.nase.org/NASE/)

Good information, great links.

Entrepreneurial Edge Online
(http://www.edgeonlin.com/)

Yet another very well-done entrepreneurial website. In addition to all the standard information about everything from market analysis to financial rations, this site has many helpful training modules for the beginning entrepreneur.

AIMC: Working from Home Center
(http://aimc.com/aimc/homework.html)

American Homebusiness Association
(http://www.homebusiness.com/)

Business@Home
(http://www.gohome.com)

The above three websites offer assorted information and links for people operating, or starting, home businesses.

Entrepreneur Magazine's Small Business Square
(http:www.entrepreneurmag.com)

Includes a library of over 2,500 articles, all kinds of information and tips, and some great links.

Worldprofit Mail Complex
(http://www.worldprofit.com)

This is Jeffrey Lant's web mail. Check it out to see how the web is used by a marketing machine.

The Tiny Little Appendix You'll Probably Never Need: How to Deal with Failure

Rejection is part of starting a small business. You learn not to take it personally, and let it go. Failure is different. Failure is personal.

At the moment we're writing these words, we've started seven businesses. Two of them failed miserably. That hurt.

Although it's just a remote possibility, your business might fail, too. It will hurt. Lick your wounds and think about it. Play "what if?" What would have made it more successful? What kind of business should you really have started? What would you do differently? Think about it.

Then start another business. Do it again. Starting small doesn't cost much—just don't give up. If you have to work as a temp while your new business is starting, so be it. If you have to cringe and beg for a loan, fine. Just don't give up. This is your life. Make it the life you want. Never give up.

Index

D

Data conversion, 53
Data recovery/virus control, 53
Dating coach, 93
Day care
    for children, 66
    for pets, 35
DBA, 131, 133
Delivery service, 93
Demonstrations, 174
Demo packager, 83
Depreciation, 216
Diaper cleaning, 67
Direct mail, 47, 174–78
Directories, 179, 228–29
Disk duplicating, 54
Displays, 179
Distributor, independent, 83–84
Diversification, 99
Divination, 74
Door hangers, 179

E

Eco-businesses, 70–72
Editor, 76–77
Educational programs, 180
E-mail, 183–85, 185–86
Energy efficiency consultant, 72
Equipment rental, 83
Equipment repair/fabrication, 82
Errand service, 67
Essay coaching, 77
Estate sale coordinator, 66
Events
    entertaining, 82
    hosting, 180–81
    planner, 67
Exercise coach, 75
    Expenses
    business-related, 141–44, 215
    personal, 139–40

F

Failure, dealing with, 234
Farming, 87–91
Financing, 128–30
Florist, 67
Flowers
    arranging, 67
    growing, 89
Flyers, 181
Focus groups, 122
Follow-up, 181
Foreign language instruction, 77
Frequent buyer plans, 181–82
Fund-raising, 47–48

G

Garage sale coordinator, 66
Genealogy services, 94
Gift basket business, 94
Gift buying service, 67
Gift certificates, 182
Gifts, 182–83
Grant writer, 78–79
Graphic design, 54–55
Green products retailer, 71
Guarantees, 165, 183
Guides, 95
Guiding principle
    books about, 227–28
    clusters, 13
    examples of, 5
    finding your, 3–15

H

Handyperson service, 94
Hauling service, 93
Health product sales, 75
Herb farming, 89
Home design consultant, 68
Home office deduction, 217–18
Horse services, 35
House cleaning, 66
HPS (High Probability Selling), 193–95, 230